Global Art

GLOBAL ART

Activities, Projects and Inventions
From Around the World

MaryAnn F. Kohl and Jean Potter

Illustrations by Rebecca Van Slyke

gryphon house

Beltsville, Maryland

In memory of my Yugoslavian grandparents,
Katherine Benkovic Matovich and George Matovich,
Samuel Benič and Catherine Brazdic Benič

Jean Potter

In memory of Alice U. Kohl,
my children's grandmother and my dear mother-in-law,
who made the best pie crust in the world.

Mary Ann Kohl

Copyright © 1998 MaryAnn Kohl and Jean Potter

Published by Gryphon House, Inc.
10726 Tucker Street, Beltsville, MD 20705

World Wide Web: http://www.ghbooks. com

Library of Congress Cataloging-in-Publication Data

Kohl, Mary Ann F.
    Global art : activities, projects, and Inventions from around the world / MaryAnn F. Kohl and Jean Potter ; Illustrations by Rebecca Van Slyke.
        p.   cm.
    Includes Indexes.
    ISBN 0-87659-190-X
    1. Art--Study and teaching (Elementary)--United States.
    2. Education, Elementary--United States--Activity programs.
    3. Multiculturalism in art.   I. Potter, Jean, 1947-   .   II. Title.
    N362.K66 1998
    372.5'044'0973--dc21   98-3273
                                                        CIP

Table of Contents

▼To respect the origins of many of the projects, inventions and activities in this book, they have been organized within each continent by country or cultural group.

Chapter Four 73

EUROPE

Chapter Five 111

NORTH AMERICA

Welcome!

What is special about *Global Art*?

Global Art is an activity book filled with over 130 art ideas from around the world. Some are based on customs, some on celebrations, others on discoveries or inventions and still others on native materials used in open artistic expression. *Global Art* combines the fun and creativity of art with the mysteries of history, the lure of geography and the diversity of the cultures of the world.

Process, Not Product

The projects in *Global Art* allow children to explore the world through art with a process, not a product, approach to artistic outcome. In other words, it is the process of exploring and creating, rather than the finished product, that is most important for the young artist. The activities leave room for the artist to use imagination and exploration, keys to creativity.

The world of art is a wide and wonderful experience!

Why is art that explores the history and geography of countries important for children?

We live in a world of global connections. Children hear about world events; they go to school with children from around the world; they use products that are made all over the globe. Yet, children learn best when experiences are concrete and meaningful to their everyday lives. By using hands-on, down-to-earth art experiences, children learn about the myriad people who have shaped the world from the past to the present. By exploring and interpreting each art activity, children become familiar with people and their customs in a way that is meaningful to them. The cultural aspects of the art activities may inspire and motivate the young artist. Through art, children discover how geography, history and time link all people together, how we are different, how we are alike and how we are all connected to the cultural heritage of the past. Through a variety of art experiences, children explore the contributions of different cultures. Activities in *Global Art* are a springboard for art as a language of understanding and respect for the diverse human spirit the world over.

Using the Icons

On each page of *Global Art*, there are icons in the upper corner of the page to assist the young artist and the supervising adult in project selection. These icons are suggestions only. Keep in mind the interests of the artists, and approach each activity on its own merit, no matter the age or experience level.

Experience level

The experience icon assists in choosing a project based on how easy or difficult it might be.

 one star for the beginning artist with little experience

 two stars for artists with some art experience

 three stars for the more experienced artist

Age and skill do not necessarily go hand-in-hand; therefore, the experience icon flags which projects are for new or beginning level artists, mid-level artists with some experience and advance-level artists with greater experience.

Suggestion: Read the entire activity first, then collect all the materials before starting.

Art techniques

The art technique icons shows which art medium is primarily used in the project. Many projects incorporate more than one art medium; the icon shows the primary one.

 painting   drawing

 sculpture   collage

 construction   printing

Planning and preparation

The planning and preparation icons show how easy or difficult it is to prepare for the activity.

 1 all materials are likely to be found in your home or school

 2 all materials are familiar but may need to be found or purchased before beginning the activity

 3 requires materials that may be unfamiliar, but easily gotten, such as beeswax (art supply store) or window screen (hardware store)

Africa

Today Africa is a continent of modern cities, vast deserts and deep jungles, giving it some of the most diverse cultures and art in the world. Most African art comes from everyday life, from fabric designs to woven basketry. The art of Africa expresses tribal life and tradition. In fact, many of Africa's ancient arts and crafts are thriving and commonly in use today. Young artists will explore many African tribes and countries through art, such as: Nuba Face Painting, Ashanti Printed Cloth, Senufo Drum Decoration, Egyptian Filigree Jewelry, Cameroon Animal masks, Malawi Galimoto Scepters, Ghana Ilukeres Fly Whisks, Yoruba Metal Casting, Nigerian Royalty Hangings and Congo Ivory. Over 20 art explorations for young artists will invite them to meet African nations up close through their jewelry, fabric, face paint and other exciting art works.

Selected Bibliography

Abiyoyo by Pete Seeger (Simon & Schuster, 1994)

Ashanti to Zulu: African Traditions by Margaret Musgrove (Dial, 1976)

Bimwili and the Zimwi by Verna Aardema (Dial, 1985)

Boundless Grace by Mary Hoffman (Dial, 1995)

A Country Far Away by Nigel Gray (Orchard, 1989)

How Many Spots Does a Leopard Have and Other Tales by Julius Lester (Scholastic, 1989)

Jambo Means Hello by Muriel Feelings (Dial, 1985)

Shadow by Blaise Cendrars (Simon & Schuster, 1982)

Central Africa

A is for Africa by Ifeoma Onyefulu (Dutton, 1993)

Chidi Only Likes Blue by Ifeoma Onyefulu (Penguin, 1996)

Emeka's Gift by Ifeoma Onyefulu (Dutton, 1995)

East Africa

Bringing the Rain to Kapiti Plain: A Nandi Tale by Verna Aardema (Dial, 1981)

Moja Means One by Muriel Feelings (Penguin, 1971)

The Village of Round and Square Houses by Ann Grifalconi (Little Brown, 1986)

Egypt

The Day of Ahmed's Secret by Florence Parry Heide (Lothrop, 1990)

The Hundredth Name by Shulamith Levey Oppenheim (Boyd Mills, 1995)

Magid Fasts for Ramadan by Mary Matthews (Clarion, 1996)

Mummies Made in Egypt by Aliki (HarperCollins, 1979)

Ghana

A Story, A Story by Gail E. Haley (Simon & Schuster, 1970)

Malawi

Galimoto by Karen Lynn Williams (Morrow, 1991)

South Africa

Darkness and the Butterfly by Ann Grifalconi (Little Brown, 1987)

The Day Gogo Went to Vote by Elinor Batezat Sisulu (Little Brown, 1996)

The Dove by Dianne Stewart (Greenwillow, 1993)

Not So Fast, Songololo by Niki Daly (Simon & Schuster, 1986)

West Africa

Anansi the Spider: A Tale from the Ashanti by Gerald McDermott (Holt, 1972)

Kente Colors by Debbi Chocolate (Walker, 1996)

Mufaro's Beautiful Daughters: An African Tale by John Steptoe (Lothrop, 1987)

Why Mosquitoes Buzz in People's Ears: A West African Tale by Verna Aardema (Dial, 1975)

Zoma the Rabbit by Gerald McDermott (Harcourt Brace, 1992)

Sandpaper Printed Cloth

caution   drawing   preparation   some experience

Young artists create their own elaborate cloth patterns using sandpaper and crayons, permanently ironing the crayon wax into fabric.

Materials

sandpaper
crayons
old scissors
piece of light colored cotton fabric
thick pad of newspapers
newsprint
old iron set on low

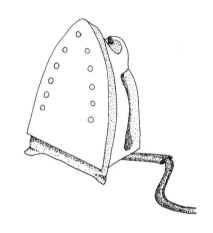

Process

1. Draw a shape on the back of the sandpaper.
2. Cut the shape out of the sandpaper.
3. Draw other shapes on additional sheets of sandpaper and cut those out too.
4. Arrange the shapes under the fabric with the sandpaper face up.
5. With crayons, randomly color over the muslin and watch the symbols appear from the shapes underneath. Use many different bright colors.
▲ Note: Holding the fabric (and sandpaper pieces) in place with masking tape will make crayoning easier.
6. Move the shapes around to make connecting patterns.
7. When the coloring is complete, place the cloth on the pad of newspapers, crayon side down.
8. Cover the cloth with a clean sheet of newsprint to protect the old iron.
9. With adult supervision, iron the cloth to melt the crayon into the fabric and set the designs.

ASHANTI, GHANA

Did you know?

The Ashanti people are the largest ethnic group in the West African country of Ghana. Most of the Ashanti live in south-central Ghana in the Ashanti Region. Ashanti weavers are famous for producing colorful kente cloth. The Ashanti decorate fabric by painting and stamping patterns on them. Each cloth is brilliantly colored and contains intricate designs that represent their heritage.

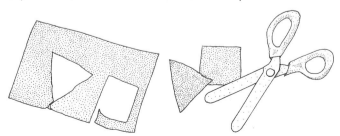

experienced   preparation   sculpture

Animal Masks

BAMILEKE, CAMEROON

Did you know?

The Bamileke people of Cameroon use animal designs in their mask making. A mask decorated with a geometric pattern of white bead triangles might represent the spots of the leopard's coat, which the Bamileke believe refers to royalty. The frog is a sign of fertility, or the ability to have many children. Symbols that show strength, intelligence, cunning and status (one's importance in society) are meant to bring luck and prosperity to the people who wear the masks.

Young artists create masks with plaster of Paris in a sandbox mold and decorate them with their own personal symbols of importance.

Materials

sand
water in a container
spoons, sticks, dull knives and other sculpting utensils
plaster of Paris
mixing container and mixing spoon
colored markers

Process

1. Find an area of sand in a sandbox or at the beach that is smooth and firm or patted down, or put some sand in a plastic dish pan. Moisten the sand well with water.
2. Trace and dig a hole in the sand the desired shape of the mask. An oval is a good shape, but it can be any shape.
3. Moisten the sand again, and be careful not to damage the shape.
4. Sculpt areas in the sand to make the face of the mask more interesting. These can simply be designs or indentations.
5. In the container, mix the plaster of Paris according to package directions. Pour the plaster of Paris over the mask form in the sand.
▲ Note: Never rinse plaster down the drain or a serious clog may occur. Let plaster dry and toss the left-over bits out in the trash or add to a garden.
6. Let the plaster dry, then lift it gently out of the sand. Brush the excess sand off the plaster.
7. Dry some more. When completely dry, use colored markers to decorate the mask with symbols to represent animals.
8. Display the mask on a table, hang it up or set on a shelf as a decoration.

Plaster of Paris

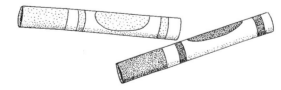

14   GLOBAL ART

Colorful Baskets

Young artists glue fabric scraps around a soup bowl to make a basket similar to those found in Zambia.

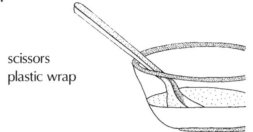

Materials

white glue, water, plastic spoon
small soup bowls
colorful cotton fabric

scissors
plastic wrap

Process

1. Make a mixture of half white glue and half water in one of the bowls. Mix well. Set aside.
2. Cut the fabric into 2" (5 cm) squares. Set aside.
3. Place a bowl upside down on the work surface. Cover the outside of the bowl with plastic wrap.
4. Dip the squares of fabric in the glue and water mixture. Squeeze off the excess water by slipping the squares between two fingers.
5. Press the fabric squares onto the plastic wrap-covered bowl.
6. Follow the same procedure of dipping fabric squares and placing them on the plastic wrap, overlapping them three or four times to cover the entire bowl.
7. Let the fabric-covered bowl dry overnight, or several days if necessary.
8. When completely dry, take the fabric bowl form off the plastic wrap.
9. If the edges are ragged, use scissors to trim and clean up the edges. The bowl can be used as a basket or container, but it will not hold liquid or anything moist.

BAROTSE, ZAMBIA

Did you know?

The Barotse tribe in Zambia uses woven grasses to make their coiled baskets. Other cultures make similar kinds of baskets from different types of materials, including grasses.

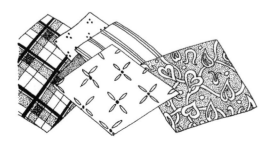

Decorative Necklaces

CENTRAL AFRICA

Did you know?

For hundreds of years, Central African women have been wearing beautiful metal collar necklaces. These necklaces have been copied by many, including cloth versions worn today.

Young artists use paper plates to make necklaces like those worn in Central Africa.

Materials

large paper plates
markers and crayons
scissors

Process

1. Study the paper plate ribbing.
2. Color only the ribbing using different designs, shapes and colors.
3. Snip through the outside ring of the paper plate to get to the circular inside.
4. Cut away the entire inside circle of the plate so only the ribbing is left.
5. Slip the colored paper necklace around the neck to wear.

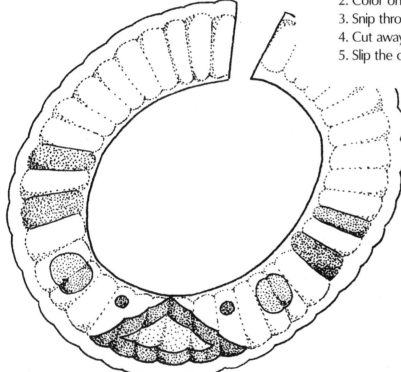

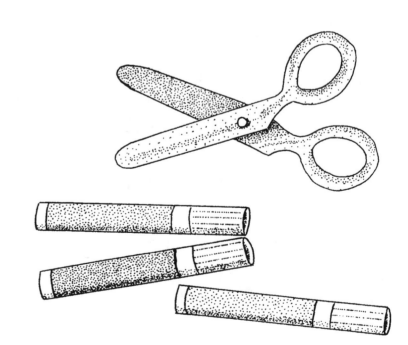

Dogon Door Decor

Young artists create modern-day door hangings similar to those of the Dogon people of Africa.

Materials

wooden board about 6"x 12" (15 cm x 30 cm)
pencil
colored markers
natural materials such as

feathers	grasses	weeds
leaves	shells	pebbles

glue
electric drill, adult help required
string

Process

1. Use the pencil to draw designs on the smooth side of the wood to symbolize something important to the artist. For example, draw a favorite sport, a pet, a family member, a religious symbol, a home or car.
2. Use the colored markers to color in the designs and symbols.
3. Decorate the wood with other natural materials by gluing them on the board.
4. With adult help, drill two holes about an inch, or 3 centimeters, from the top on both sides of the wood. Lace the string through the holes and tie a knot in the back to make a hanger.
5. Ask permission to hang the decorative door plaque on a door of the house, classroom, clubhouse or even a fence or mailbox.

Variation

✓ Place self-hardening clay on a table and roll it out with a rolling pin. Use a pencil to carve pictures and designs in the clay. Make holes at the top and lace string through the holes to hang it on a door when dry.

DOGON, MALI

Did you know?

A Dogon village in Mali has buildings for storing grain called granaries, which are very important to the existence of Dogon villagers. Because of this importance, Dogon people often decorate the doors of their granaries to show respect.

Many Dogon people live as they have for centuries, without changing ancient custom or traditions. Many wear traditional clothing and live in traditional homes.

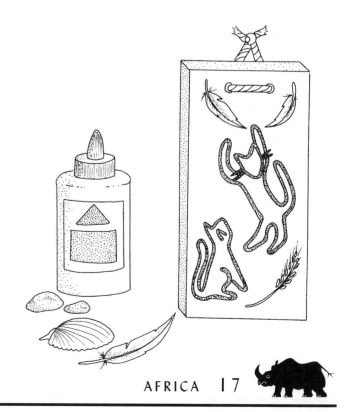

Royal Jewelry

EGYPT

Did you know?

Ancient Egyptian jewelry was breathtakingly beautiful. Jewelry was considered highly valuable property of the royal families. The Egyptians believed that the dead were going on a journey to another world; therefore, all of their jewelry was put into their tombs with them so they could have it with them when they reached their destination.

Young artists make beaded necklaces using clay, toothpicks and string.

Materials

clay (non-bake, air-hardening variety)
round toothpick
string long enough for a necklace
clean newsprint

Process

1. Take a small amount of clay and roll it into a ball, cylinder or oblong shape. Lentil shapes can be made by rolling round beads and then flattening them. Make as many beads as desired.
2. Stick a toothpick through the longest part of each bead to make a hole through the center of the bead.
3. With the point of the toothpick, etch designs in the beads to resemble hieroglyphic writing or other ideas.
4. Lace the beads on the string as each one is completed.
5. Spread the string of beads out on a sheet of clean newsprint to dry. Let the clay dry completely, usually for several days. Turn the beads occasionally so they won't stick to the string as they dry.
6. Tie the necklace around the neck and wear the royal beads, or give them as a gift.

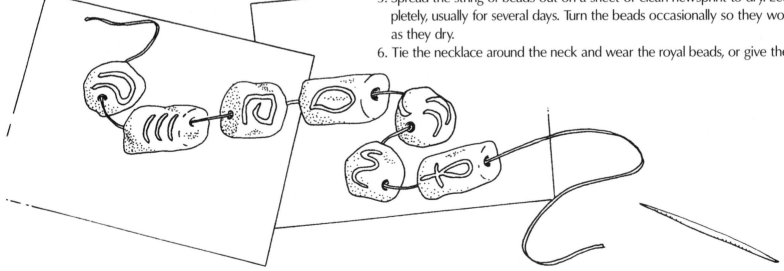

Filigree Jewelry

caution

sculpture

2 preparation

some experience

Young artists curl, wrap and twist copper or brass wire into unusual pieces of jewelry. Leftover colorful telephone cable wire can also be used and is easily cut with scissors.

Materials

thin and heavy brass or copper wire
wire cutter and file
colored telephone cable wire, optional
needle-nose pliers
dowel
hammer, optional
metal slab, optional

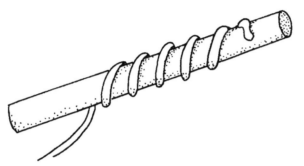

Process

1. Cut wire to desired lengths for working the filigree. Smooth the pointed ends of the wire with a file before beginning design work. Colored telephone cable wires can be substituted for the copper or brass wire.
2. Use the needle-nose pliers to experiment with shapes and forms desired. Some examples of filigree wire techniques are:
   ✔ To make a curl, wrap the wire around a dowel. Slip the wire off the dowel carefully to maintain the curl.
   ✔ To make earrings, **remember the earrings should hang over the ear and will not be placed through the ear**. Use the wire cutter to cut two pieces of wire the same size, about 5–8" (13–20 cm). Leave about 2" (5 cm) of wire to hang the earring **over** the ear.
   ▲ Caution: NEVER put the wire through anyone's ear!
   ✔ To make the wire flat, pound the wire on the metal slab with a hammer until the wire is thin.
   ✔ Other suggestions for bending wire into jewelry are shown in the illustrations.
3. Wear the jewelry or give as a gift to someone special.

EGYPT

Did you know?

The custom of wearing jewelry as ornaments on the body has been practiced for as long as people have populated the earth. One of the art techniques of the Egyptians was called filigree, the art of twisting or curling wire into shapes or objects to create jewelry, from pins and bracelets to brooches and earrings. Filigree decoration was also practiced in ancient Greece, China and Egypt as well as by the Etruscans in ancient Italy.

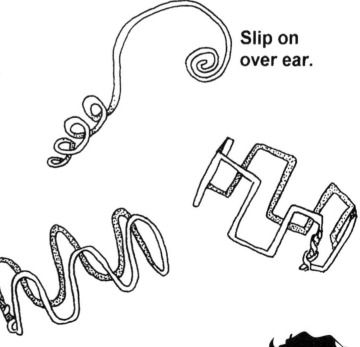

Slip on over ear.

Scarab Stones

EGYPT

Did you know?

Centuries ago, the Egyptian people considered the scarabaeid beetle to be sacred. Representations of the beetle were made of ceramics or stone and were said to symbolize the soul of Man.

Young artists make beetles and other scarabs using round stones decorated with tempera paints.

Materials

smooth round stones, small to medium
soap and water
towel
tempera paints and paintbrushes
hair spray

Process

1. Wash the rounded stone with soap and water.
2. Dry the stone with a towel.
3. Paint the clean stone one solid color. Dry.
4. After the first coating of paint is dry, paint lines and eyes on the stone so it resembles a beetle or other bug.
5. After the paint has dried, spray the painted stone with hair spray to give it a glossy coating.

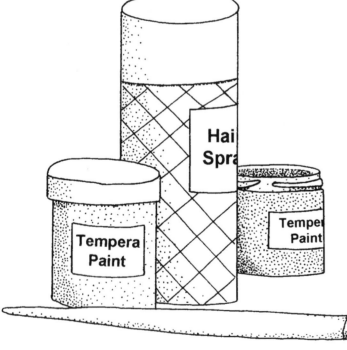

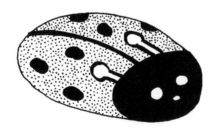

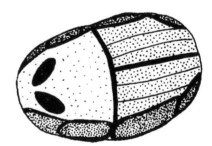

Ancient Etchings

caution   drawing   preparation   some experience

Young artists depict a modern day scene by etching symbols in clay, using the same techniques as those done thousands of years ago in Egypt.

Materials

1 cup (250 ml) baking soda
½ cup (125 ml) cornstarch
⅔ cup (150 ml) warm water
saucepan and stove
bread board

wax paper or other paper for drying clay
large nail for scratching designs
shoe polish and rag
shellac or clear nail polish, optional

Process

1. Prepare the play clay: Mix the baking soda and cornstarch in a saucepan. Add the water and stir until smooth. With adult help, put the pan on the stove on medium heat, boil and stir the mixture until it is the consistency of mashed potatoes. Pour onto a board to cool. Knead.

2. Spread the clay out on wax paper. Press into a large rectangular or oval shape, or into several individual rectangles or ovals.

3. Let dry. This clay hardens quickly and can be used the same day.

4. When dry, use a nail to scratch and etch designs or hieroglyphics into the surface of the hard play clay. Think of symbols that might represent the artist, such as

soccer ball	horse	musical note
bicycle	pet	book

Authentic hieroglyphic symbols, such as those shown in the illustration, may also be etched.

5. Rub a little shoe polish over the etched clay rectangle with a rag to make it look old and fill in some of the etchings.

6. If desired, the play clay may be covered with shellac or clear nail polish when dry to give it a shiny, protective coating.

EGYPT

Did you know?

The ancient tombs of pharaohs and queens were decorated with drawings depicting scenes of daily living. The drawings are known as hieroglyphics, a type of written language made up of little symbols and pictures.

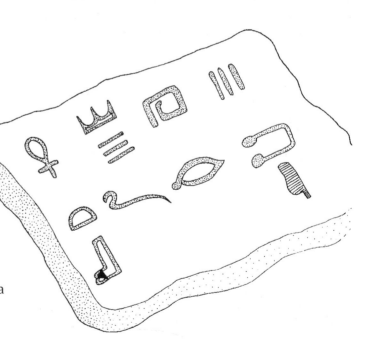

easier preparation construction caution

Ilukeres Fly Whisks

GHANA

Did you know?

The kings of an Ashanti village in Ghana carried Ilukeres made to denote royalty and to fan away flying insects. They were generally made from animal tails and had engraved golden handles. They could be flicked back and forth to scare away flies.

Young artists construct a fly whisk from cardboard tubes and strips of paper to carry in a most royal fashion. The artists may enjoy reading A *Story, A Story* by Gail Haley (Atheneum, 1970).

Materials

crepe paper and other paper
scissors
tape or stapler
cardboard tube
cord or string
colored markers

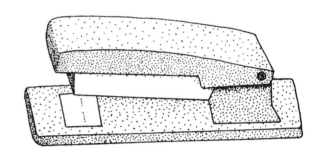

Process

1. Cut several strips of crepe paper about 5″ (13 cm) long.
2. Cut several strips of other papers about 5″ (13 cm) long.
3. Gather the crepe paper strips together with other strips of paper. Tape or staple them to one end of the cardboard tube.
4. Attach a loop of cord or string to the opposite end of the tube so the Ilukeres can be carried.
5. Decorate the handle with the markers to symbolize the royalty of the person carrying it.
6. Whisk away flies, real or imaginary.

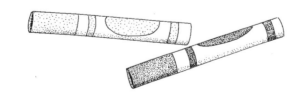

 22 GLOBAL ART

Substitute Ivory

Ivory is taken from the tusks of elephants that are often killed illegally for their ivory tusks. As a result, the world is losing these precious animals. Therefore, anything made from ivory should not be purchased. Young artists create forms carved in substitute ivory by using a bar of soap and water.

Materials

resealable plastic bag
water
bar of soap
nail
string

Process

1. Fill the bag half full with water.
2. Put the bar of soap in the bag.
3. Place the bag on a flat surface so that the water just covers the soap.
4. Let the soap soak in the water for 1 or 2 hours. From time to time, feel the soap through the bag. When it is soft on both sides, it is ready to use.
5. Take the soap out of the bag and squeeze and mold it by hand to make a shape or figurine.
6. Poke a hole through the top of the figure with a nail and lace a piece of string through the top. Then let it dry.
7. Hang the soap figure through a belt or through a belt loop and dance with it hanging from the belt.

LEGA, CONGO

Did you know?

The Lega people of eastern Congo created small ivory figures. These figures were often displayed together or used in dances. In dances, the figures would be tied to the dancer's forehead, chest, arm, leg, or loincloth. When a member of the tribe or a tribal leader dies, his figurine is passed on to family members of similar status.

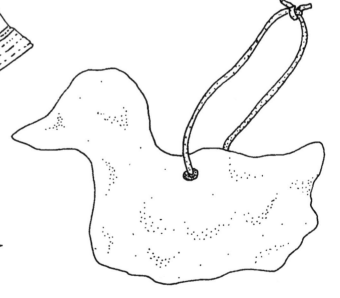

Galimoto Sculptures

some experience | preparation | 2 | sculpture

MALAWI

Did you know?

The children of Malawi collect scraps of wire to twist into toys. They especially like to bend the wire into different shapes of cars and other vehicles. Galimoto means "car" in the national language of Malawi which is Chichewa.

Young artists bend wire to make galimoto sculptures or other sculpture shapes. Read *Galimoto* by Karen Lynn Williams (Morrow, 1991).

Materials

plastic-coated colored wire (recycled from scrap telephone cable)
scissors
sticks

Process

1. Use the wire pieces to bend into shapes of cars or other ideas.
2. Add different colors of wire to twist around the shapes to add design features and details.
3. Twist a piece of wire around a stick and attach the wire sculpture to it.
4. Place the stick into the dirt, grass or a garden to hold the sculpture in place.

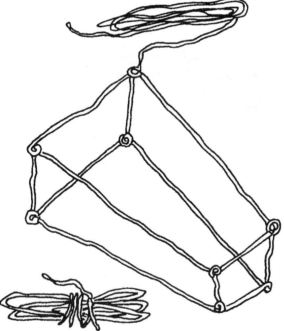

Royalty Hangings

Young artists make plaques from plaster of Paris using symbols to represent the objects, ideas and characteristics that are important to each of them and their families.

Materials

plaster of Paris
aluminum pie pan
collected materials, such as
   leaves, twigs, flowers, feathers, shells, play jewels, beads, buttons, lace, glitter, sequins and other special collected things
colored markers
glue
string

disposable container, water and mixing spoon
stick

Process

1. Mix the plaster of Paris in a disposable container with a spoon according to directions on the package. Quickly pour the plaster into the aluminum pie pan.
▲ Note: Never rinse plaster down the drain or a serious clog may occur. Let plaster dry and toss the leftover bits out in the trash or add to a garden.
2. Poke the stick all the way through the plaster in the pie pan so it makes two holes where the hanger string will be placed later.
3. Place the collected materials into the plaster making a decorative design in the plaque. Work quickly so the plaster doesn't dry before finishing.
4. Let the plaster dry for several minutes.
5. Continue decorating the plaque with the colored markers, glitter and sequins. Use symbols that represent the objects, ideas and characteristics important to the artists. Some ideas of symbols to draw might be the sun, smiley face, dog, ball, fishing pole, car, or holiday symbols like bunny, tree, menorah, pumpkin, firecracker, flag, heart or basket.
6. Let the plaster dry a little more, then pop it out of the pie pan. Slip the string through the hole to make a hanger. Hang the plaque on the entry door to a home, classroom, clubhouse or friend's house.

NIGERIA

Did you know?

In Nigeria and other African nations, beautiful and elaborate art objects have been created for royal courts. One way to show that royalty lived in a particular dwelling was to make a plaque and attach it to the wooden pillars of the royal palace entryway. Traditionally, the art of these kingdoms was commissioned by governments and served the purpose of enhancing and maintaining the status of rulers.

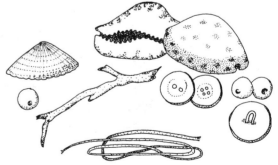

Mud Painting

SENUFO, IVORY COAST

Did you know?

The elaborate art created by the Senufo tribe of the Ivory Coast of West Africa includes mud painting. The Senufo stretch fabric tightly on a wooden board and artists paint pictures of animals on it using shiny black mud. The fabric is used to make traditional clothing. Hunters wore the fabric as camouflage because the black and white pattern is difficult to see among the trees and undergrowth. The animal figures were symbolic protection against danger and were believed to help the hunter bring in a big catch.

Young artists create mud paintings (particularly on a rainy day!) using embroidery hoops and actual mud.

Materials

unbleached muslin
embroidery hoops
water
spoon

bowl
mud or clay
paintbrush

Process

1. Put the muslin in the embroidery hoop, stretching the fabric tightly. Set aside.
2. Place a few tablespoons of mud in a bowl. Add a little water to thin.
3. Mix the mud or clay with the water until it is thinned and can be painted with a brush. It does not need to be completely dissolved, but the water needs to be heavily colored.
4. Dip the paintbrush in the muddy water.
5. Use the muddy water to paint animals or other designs on the muslin.
6. Dry the muslin. Remove from the embroidery hoop, or display the fabric in the hoop.

Variation

✓ For a larger variation of the embroidery hoop, stretch the fabric over the edges of a board until tight. Paint a larger design on the stretched fabric.

Drum Decoration

construction   preparation   beginner

Young artists make decorated drums and then dance to a rhythm.

Materials

oatmeal box with lid, clean
construction paper
colored markers
white glue
string
miscellaneous collectible, decorative materials, such as

buttons	feathers
dried flowers	beads
sewing spools	leaves

Process

1. Use the markers to decorate the construction paper using symbols that might have special meaning. The symbols should stand for something important to the artist. Some ideas for symbols might be the sun, a fishing pole, a heart, a dog, a car, a book, an apple, a bicycle or wild animals.
2. Glue the construction paper around the label area of the oatmeal box. Set aside.
3. Tie the miscellaneous materials to the string.
4. Poke a hole in the sides of the oatmeal box and attach the materials to the box so they hang off the drum.
5. Use the box as a drum in a rhythmic dance or simply to create music by tapping on the ends.

SENUFO, IVORY COAST

Did you know?

Drums are used in masking ceremonies (ceremonies using masks) and to communicate with other tribes and villages. Drums give the beat for dancing and also tell the dancers when to change their steps. Animal forms drawn on the drums of the Senufo tribe have special meanings. The Senufo people believe that the hornbill was the first animal on earth and that it acts as a messenger between humans and the gods, and that the alligator is a symbol of fertility.

some experience · **preparation** · **construction**

Bambulina Hanging

SOUTH AFRICA

Did you know?

South Africans make beautiful, brightly colored weavings called bambulinas. These weavings are loosely woven materials that are highly decorated and often used as wall hangings.

Young artists create bambulina weavings with burlap and yarn to enjoy as a wall hanging or even a table runner.

Materials

½ yard (½ m) burlap
scissors
dowel or stick
tape or stapler
yarn in different colors
½ yard (½ m) ball fringe (pompoms) in different colors, optional

Process

1. Cut a piece of burlap in a square any size. Cut off the selvage edge so all the edges are raw.
2. Use tape or a stapler to attach the burlap to the dowel or stick. Cut a piece of yarn and attach to the dowel to hang the burlap.
3. Look at the fabric. Pull the end of a thread completely out of the weave. Remove enough string to make a space about 2″ (5 cm) wide.
4. Move down the square a little. Repeat the removing of threads.
5. Do this again a little farther down the square. (See the illustration.)
6. Cut long and short lengths of several colors of yarn.
7. Gather together several strings in the spaces where the threads were pulled. Tie short pieces of yarn around the burlap strings in little triangle shaped gathers.
8. Continue tying the yarn onto the burlap across the spaces where threads were pulled.
9. As an optional idea and to add some additional interest, tie some fringe balls on the burlap bambulina.
10. Hang the bambulina on the wall or use as a table runner.

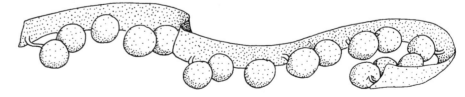

Face Painting

Young artists can paint their faces like the Southeast Nuba or create their own unique ideas.

Materials

hand lotion
tempera paints and paintbrushes
little dishes, 1 for each color

mirror
tissues and cotton balls
old face towel

Process

TRADITIONAL SOUTHEAST NUBA PAINTING

1. Mix several drops of tempera paint with a little hand lotion in little dishes, each color in a separate dish.
▲ Note: This makes a nice face paint that is easily removed with tissues.
2. Draw a black outline of a triangle around each eye and down the cheeks.
3. Take yellow-brown paint and fill in the triangles.
▲ Note: Be sure to keep paint away from eyes, eyelashes and eyelids.

FACE PAINTING

1. Set up the mirror on a table with the mixed paints, brushes and tissues.
2. Look into the mirror while painting designs on the cheeks, nose, forehead, chin and around the eyes and mouth. Be careful not to get paint in the eyes or mouth.
3. To remove paint, hop in the shower or tub and go for a total scrubbing. Or, if bathing facilities are limited, soak tissues or cotton balls in hand lotion and rub gently to remove. An old face towel can remove the remainder of paint with lotion.

SOUTHEAST NUBA, SUDAN

Did you know?

A small group of people called Southeast Nuba live in the remote mountains of the Sudan, a country in northeast Africa. The men of this culture paint their faces in intricate designs. They consider painting their faces a work of art and each day they create face painting designs just as an artist would paint on canvas.

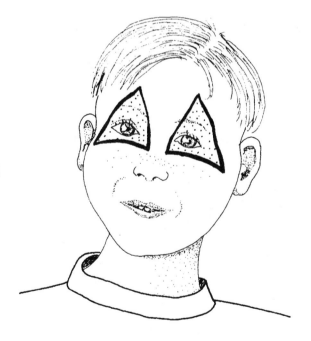

Grigri Charms

TRADITIONAL AFRICA

Did you know?

Many years ago, grigris were worn by people in tribes and countries all over Africa. Grigris could be made of leather, ivory, fibers, bone, metal and sometimes gold, and they were thought to have magical qualities of luck, protection and happiness. Today, grigris are worn in North Africa where they are made from leather with printed symbols and designs on them.

Young artists construct grigri charms from cork and suspend them from a string to wear as a necklace for good luck and happiness.

Materials

thin cork wall tile or bulletin board sheeting
colored markers
scissors
paper punch
string or cord, 24" (60 cm) long

Process

1. Design and color a grigri symbol on the sheet of cork. Any shape or design will do.
2. Cut out the grigri symbol with scissors.
3. Punch a hole in the top of the cork symbol with the paper punch.
4. Thread the string through the hole to make a necklace.
5. Tie it around the neck and wear as a charm for good luck and happiness.

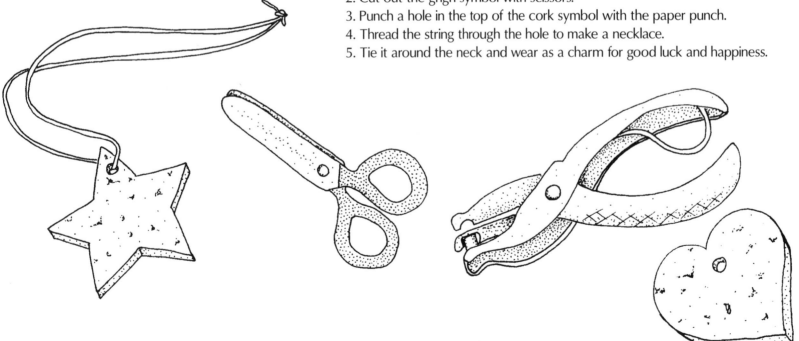

Animal Abstracts

caution   construction   preparation   beginner

Young artists make animal abstracts from objects in nature.

Materials

twigs

natural materials found in the environment, such as

   sticks   grasses   pine cones

   weeds   stones   leaves

glue (preferably hot glue-gun with adult supervision)

Process

1. Study the twigs closely. Decide which shapes may work best to form an animal likeness.
2. Arrange all of the twigs and other materials together.
3. Glue the materials together to make an animal abstract. Legs can be extra long, noses can be wiggly and wavy and other exaggerations can be made to make funny creatures.
4. Glue on the other materials to highlight portions of the animal's body, such as little stones for eyes or grasses or leaves for a tail.

Variation

✓ Make people instead of animals. Add fabric scraps and sewing trims for clothing.

TRADITIONAL AFRICA

Did you know?

Art objects from Africa often look the way they do for specific reasons. Much African art is not intended to look realistic. Traditional African artists are more interested in depicting an ideal or the world of the unseen, such as things from the imagination, from the spirit world or from mythological or religious beliefs; therefore, their art is often abstract and not realistic.

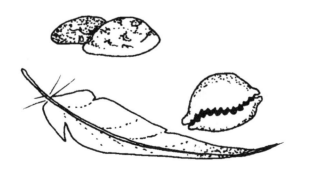

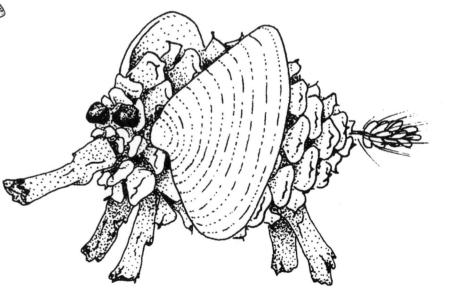

Wood Burning

WEST AFRICA

Did you know?

The people of West Africa have been carving wooden masks and other objects for generations. Woodcarving is a very old art form. Woodburning is another art technique accomplished by drawing on wood with a burning hot stick or pieces of coal.

Young artists draw a meaningful picture then burn it into wood using a soldering iron with adult supervision.

Materials

soldering iron, with one-on-one adult assistance
pine board about 6" x 8" (15 cm x 20 cm)
fine grain sandpaper
pencil
cloth
paint lacquer

Process

▲ Caution: A great deal of care and caution must be used with this activity. One-on-one adult assistance is essential.

1. Pre-heat the soldering iron and keep aside in a safe place.
2. Smooth the pine board with the sandpaper where the design will be burned. The wood must be perfectly smooth.
3. First use a pencil to draw a simple design or picture on the sanded pine.
4. With one-on-one adult assistance, take the heated soldering iron and carefully and slowly draw it over the pencil lines to burn them into the pine.
5. Continue burning the wood until the picture is complete.
6. Turn off the soldering iron, and have an adult put it in a safe place.
7. To add shine and make the design show better, wipe the wood-burned design with a cloth dipped in paint lacquer.

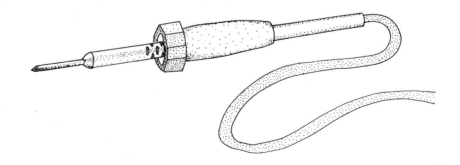

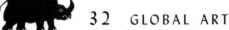

Metal Casting

Young artists use aluminum foil and plaster of Paris to explore the art of metal casting.

Materials

aluminum foil
box lid
plaster of Paris
water, spoon, bowl
tempera paints and brushes
wooden block and glue, optional

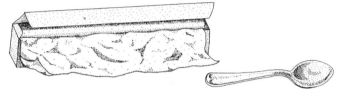

YORUBA, NIGERIA

Did you know?

Yoruba kings were called Orni. They lived more than 500 years ago in the capital city of Nigeria, Africa. Their artists were masters at casting or forming bronze sculptures.

Process

1. Tear off four to five sheets of foil and stack them on top of one another.
2. Mold the foil into an open shape. Shapes that work best are similar to those shown in the illustrations such as a bowl.
3. Place the molded foil shape into the box lid.
4. Mix the plaster of Paris in a bowl according to package directions, stirring with a spoon.
5. Before the plaster can harden, pour it into the foil mold. Let dry for several minutes.
▲ Note: Never rinse plaster of Paris down the drain or a serious clog may occur. Let plaster dry and toss the dried-out plaster in the trash or add to a garden.
6. When the plaster is dry enough to handle without breaking, remove the plaster shape from the foil. Dry completely.
7. Paint the plaster shape. Dry.
8. As an optional idea, glue the shape to a block of wood for a stand and display in a place of honor.

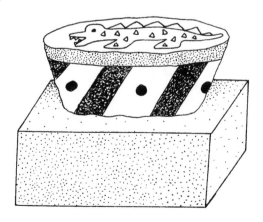

Tie-Dye Top

YORUBA, NIGERIA & WEST AFRICA

Did you know?

Tie-dye is a fabric-dying art form that flourishes throughout West Africa from Cameroon to Liberia to Nigeria. Colors and patterns are unique within each country and within each tribe. For example, the Yoruba of Nigeria dye their fabrics with indigo and then, when dry, sprinkle more indigo on the fabric and pound the cloth with wooden mallets to make the fabric shine.

There are many ways to tie-dye. Young artists begin by tying a rectangular shaped piece of fabric in knots and then submerging it in a strong dye bath to make a tie-dyed top to wear. When the knots are untied, wonderful patterns and designs are discovered.

Materials

old cotton sheet or muslin fabric
scissors
latex gloves
indigo or dark blue fabric dye
buckets
tarp or newspapers to cover floor
water
raffia, string, thread or rubber bands
iron
sewing needle
pencil

Process

1. Cut an old sheet into a rectangle that will cover the front and back of the artist.
2. Cut a V or T shaped hole in the center of the rectangle for the artist's head and neck. The rectangle should fit over the shoulders and hang down without sewing. (See illustration.)
3. Wear gloves for the next steps. Only an adult will handle the dye. Children should not handle the dye.

4. Fill a bucket with dark blue fabric dye. Place the bucket on the tarp, or on newspapers outside on the grass. Set a bucket of clear water next to the one with the blue dye.
5. Tie the rectangle in knots.
6. An adult immerses the knotted top in the dye, following the instructions on the dye box.
7. Rinse the knotted top in the clear bucket of water.
8. Dry the top overnight on newspapers. Then unknot. Wow! Look at those wonderful blue tie-dye patterns and designs!
9. Iron the top and wear. Top may be belted like a tunic.

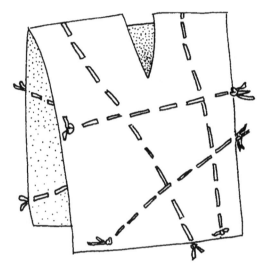

TIE-DYE—MORE COMPLICATED TYING METHOD

1. Draw some simple lines across the fabric with the pencil.
2. Thread a needle with thread or a strand of raffia. Tie a knot at one loose end.
3. Sew over the lines with the raffia strand in an in-and-out method called a running or basting stitch. When the end of a line is reached, tie another knot in the raffia, but do not sew the knot into the fabric.
4. When the lines are sewn all over, pull the knots of thread or raffia together and tie tightly.
5. Bunch up the remaining fabric and bind with rubber bands or other tied strings.
6. Following the instructions on the box, an adult immerses the sewn and bundled top into the blue dye. Children will not handle the dye step.
7. Rinse the top and dry overnight on newspapers.
8. Cut the raffia and other bindings, revealing the tie-dye patterns.
9. Iron the tie-dye top and wear. The top can be belted like a tunic, if desired.

Fabric
DYE

Chapter **2**

Antarctica

Antarctica

Almost no one travels to Antarctica except scientists and some adventurous tourists because of the ice and extremely cold weather. More than a third of Antarctica is under frozen ice! Several thousand people live there in the summer, but only a few hundred people studying the continent live there during the winter.

There are no particular arts, crafts or inventions that are part of the Antarctic culture because people come only to study and explore. Therefore, the art activities included here are to help young artists explore Antarctica's weather and climate, rather than cultures or discoveries. Antarctica remains a frozen frontier, with much yet to be learned about it. But young artists can enjoy creating and imagining through projects such as: White Sculpture, Snowy Blowy Stencil, Antarctica Snow Scene, Crystal Watercolor Snowflake, Frozen Fish Sculpture and Salt Clay Penguins.

Selected Bibliography

Life in the Polar Lands by Monica Byles (Scholastic, 1993)

The Penguin: Animal Close-Ups by Beatrice Fontanel and Valerie Tracqui (Charlesbridge, 1992)

The Polar Bear: Master of the Ice by Valerie Tracqui (Charlesbridge, 1994)

The Seal by Joelle Soler (Charlesbridge, 1992)

The Snow Queen by P. J. Lynch (Harcourt Brace, 1994)

Crystal Watercolor Snowflake

Young artists explore the effects of salt crystals on watercolor paint as they create a snowflake design.

Materials

white paper
watercolor paints
paintbrush
water in a jar, to use with paints
salt in a shallow dish

▲ Note: table salt and rock salt work in similar ways but achieve different results.

Process

1. Spread the white paper on the work surface.
2. Paint a snowflake shape, or several snowflake shapes, on the paper.
3. Take a pinch of salt and sprinkle it over the wet paint.
4. As the paint and salt dry, watch what happens to the salt crystals.

Variation

✓ Cut a snowflake out of white paper. Paint on the snowflake with watercolor paints. Then sprinkle salt on the wet snowflake for a crystallized design.

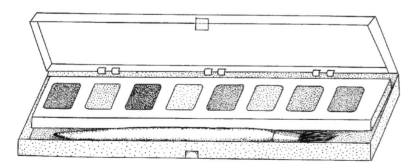

ANTARCTICA

Did you know?

Snow is composed of small crystals of frozen water. As individual crystals of ice fall through the atmosphere, they cluster together and form snowflakes. Antarctica is known for its snowy landscape from coastline to mountaintop.

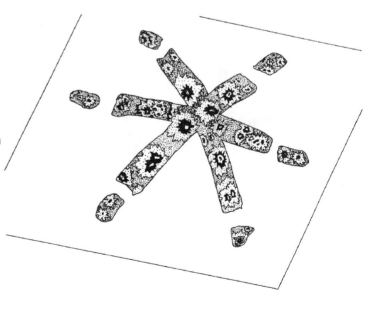

beginner
 preparation
 sculpture
! caution

Salt Clay Penguins

ANTARCTICA

Did you know?

Because it is so cold in Antarctica, the wildlife there must withstand extreme temperatures and climate. Penguins are one of the types of creatures who survive the climate best. Eighty percent of the bird inhabitants of Antarctica are penguins.

Young artists mix flour, salt and water, then use this salt clay that has been colored black, white and orange to create little penguin sculptures.

Materials

2 cups (280 g) flour
1 cup (200 g) salt
1 cup (250 ml) water
spoon
bowl
tempera paint (liquid or powdered) in orange and black
pictures of penguins
oven preheated to 250°F (130°C)

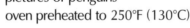

Process

1. Put the flour and salt in a bowl. Add half of the water to the mixture. Slowly and gradually add remaining water, mixing constantly.
2. After mixing well, put a little flour on the work surface. Knead the clay for 10 minutes or until the dough is smooth and firm.
▲ Note: Don't add too much water or the clay will be too sticky.
3. Break off a small ball of clay. Knead a drop of orange paint into this dough to use for the penguin's feet and beak.
4. Pinch another larger portion of the clay and knead a tiny drop of black tempera paint into it for the wings and other black areas of the penguin.
5. Leave the remaining dough white. Wash hands before step 6.
6. Use the colored dough to sculpt penguins with black wings and back, white tummy, orange beak and orange feet. Look at pictures of the different varieties of penguins to see what is realistic. Feel free to sculpt imaginary penguins, too.
7. Place the penguins on the baking tray. Ask an adult to bake them in a 250°F (130°C) oven for 1½ hours or until the penguins look hard throughout. Then cool.
8. Enjoy as figurines or sculptures.
9. Make additional sculptures if desired with leftover dough.

Snowy, Blowy Stencil

caution   painting   preparation   beginner

Young artists create snowy, blowy paintings with shoe polish and glitter to interpret the windy, snowy environment of Antarctica.

Materials

newspaper
dark blue construction paper
fern fronds or evergreen branches (if not available, cut shapes from paper that look like leaves, branches or other plants)
straight pins
toothbrush
white shoe polish
white glue thinned with water
paintbrush
silver or white glitter

Process

1. Cover the work surface with several layers of newspaper for protection. Extend the newspaper well beyond the size of the construction paper.
2. Place the construction paper on the newspaper.
3. Make an arrangement of ferns or evergreen branches one layer thick on the paper in a design. Some overlapping is fine, but not too thick. Spread the fern fronds out. Ask an adult to poke straight pins into the ferns and evergreens to pin them in place.
4. Dip the toothbrush into the white shoe polish.
5. Hold the toothbrush about 6" (15 cm) from the paper and run a thumb across the bristles several times in an upward direction until a white spattering covers the paper.
6. After achieving a fairly covered white surface, remove the branches and ferns. Set the picture aside to dry.
7. After the paint is dry, dab and lightly brush a thin layer of glue on some of the white areas to prepare for the glitter.
8. Sprinkle just enough silver glitter to give an icy sparkle to the picture. Dry again.

ANTARCTICA

Did you know?

Most precipitation in Antarctica falls as snow, amounting to as little as 2" (5 cm) in the interior and to more than 20" to 40" (50–100 cm) on the coast. Most of the precipitation comes from the cyclone-like storms that sweep into the interior from the ocean. Antarctica has the strongest sustained westerly winds on Earth.

beginner   preparation   sculpture

Soap Snow

ANTARCTICA

Did you know?

At least 96 percent of the continent of Antarctica is snow-covered. The Antarctic ice was formed from the millions of years of snow that fell on the land, layer upon layer. The weight of new snow squeezes the old snow underneath until it turns to compressed snow called firm, and then further compacts into ice. As the ice piles up, it moves toward the coast like batter spreading in a pan. The moving ice forms into glaciers, rivers of ice that flow into the sea.

Young artists mix soap flakes and water to a thick froth with a hand mixer and then squeeze on cardboard to design and sculpt a snow scene.

Materials

1 cup (250 ml) cold water
4 cups (about 500 g) of soap flakes, such as Ivory
bowl
hand mixer
pastry bag (or plastic sandwich bag)
cardboard

Process

1. Measure 1 cup cold water into a bowl.
2. With adult help while mixing with the hand mixer, add the 4 cups of soap flakes a little at a time to the cold water. Beat the soap and water just until stiff, but do not over-beat the mixture.
3. Put some of the soap mixture in the pastry bag. If a pastry bag isn't handy, fill a plastic sandwich bag and cut a small hole in the corner of the bag for the soap to escape.
4. Squeeze soapy snow designs on the cardboard. Dry until hard.
▲ Note: Do not put this soapy stuff down the drain because it will cause a serious clog.

Variation

✓ Make snow sculptures by adding 2 cups (about 250 g) soap flakes to ½ cup (125 ml) hot water. Mix with an electric mixer until stiff and moldable. Mold snow creatures, snow shapes, snow sculptures. Use beads, buttons, feathers, seeds, pipe cleaners and toothpicks to add features to the snow sculptures.

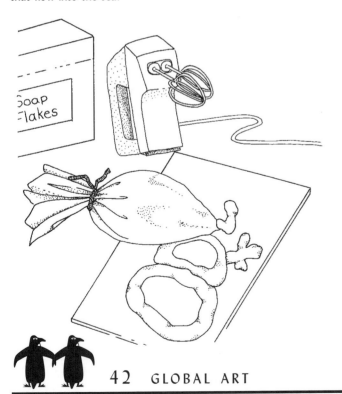

White Sculpture

sculpture   preparation   beginner

Young artists create a sculpture with all white materials as an artistic interpretation of the massive white ice sheets of Antarctica.

Materials

piece of white matte board or cardboard for the base
white-only Styrofoam materials, such as

grocery trays	packing peanuts	packing blocks

white-only materials, such as

paper	popcorn	buttons
beads	cardboard	small gift boxes

scissors
white glue
paintbrush
white or silver glitter

Process

1. Cut the Styrofoam and other white materials into different shapes and sizes, or use whole.
2. Glue the Styrofoam pieces and other white materials onto the white cardboard base, creating a white sculpture.
3. Dry until the sculpture holds together.
4. Next, brush white glue in chosen areas of the sculpture where highlighting with glitter would add sparkle.
5. Sprinkle glitter on the sculpture.
6. Dry and then display.

ANTARCTICA

Did you know?

A glacier is a large mass of slow moving, permanent ice formed on land, sometimes called an ice sheet. The great Antarctica ice sheet or glacier covers 4,826,000 sq. miles (12,500,000 sq. km). Glaciers store about 75 percent of the Earth's fresh water.

  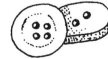

Frozen Fish Sculpture

ANTARCTICA

Did you know?

Many different fish species are found in Antarctica. These fish are small in size or few in number. The fish are food for the whales, seals, penguins, flying birds, squid and octopus that live in the waters of Antarctica.

Young artists create a sculpture with Styrofoam fish frozen in suspension.

Materials

large towel
water, plastic bowl and spoon
blue food coloring
Styrofoam grocery trays
permanent markers
scissors
materials to use as weights, such as
    lightweight paper clips, staples, rubber bands, plastic clips, tacks, string
freezer

Process

1. Spread a big towel on the work surface for spills.
2. Half fill the bowl with water. Drop a few drops of blue food coloring in the bowl and mix. Set aside.
3. Draw several fish on the Styrofoam trays with permanent markers. Color the fish brightly in different designs.
4. Cut the fish out with scissors.
5. Attach a paper clip to a fish and place it in the bowl of blue water. It should float somewhere between the surface and the bottom of the bowl. If the fish sinks, use a lighter weight paper clip. If the fish floats, add another paper clip. Work with all the fish, adding or taking away paper clips so that the fish are suspended in the bowl and look like they are swimming. It may be necessary to try other weights, such as rubber bands, staples or tacks.
6. Place the bowl and fish in the freezer for 4 hours or until frozen solid.
7. Take the bowl out of the freezer and let thaw for a few minutes.
8. Turn the bowl upside down and take the ice out of the bowl. Rinse with a little clear water, if desired, to make the ice look shiny and clear. Place the ice sculpture on the towel for a view of the frozen fish in the water.
9. When done, place the frozen fish sculpture in the sink to melt. Pick up the leftover fish and paper clips when the ice is gone. Save for another time.

Sweet Snow Sculpture

sculpture

preparation

some experience

Young artists interpret the snowy, icy environment of Antarctica by building a sculpture with sugar cubes and hard-drying icing.

Materials

2 egg whites
2 cups (240 g) confectioner's sugar
sugar cubes
bowl, mixing spoon
electric mixer, with adult help
damp towel
table knife or spreading knife
plate
plastic cake decorating figures, optional

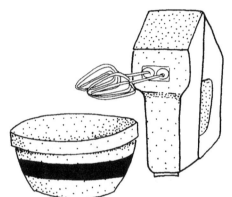

Process

1. Place the egg whites in the bowl.
2. With adult help, beat the whites with a clean electric mixer until they are frothy.
3. Mix the confectioner's sugar into the egg whites and beat until the mixture forms high peaks (about five minutes).
▲ Note: Keep the icing covered with a damp towel while not in use or between scoops when scooping out icing for the sculpture.
4. Use the icing as a glue to build a snow sculpture with the sugar cubes on a plate. Build an igloo or any other fun snowy shape by spreading the icing on the cubes.
5. Add little plastic cake decorating figures to the sculpture, if desired.
▲ Note: This sculpture will dry quickly.

ANTARCTICA

Did you know?

Antarctica is the southernmost continent located at the "bottom" of the world. It is the icy continent around the South Pole. Its elevation and its ice and snow cover make it the coldest climate on Earth. At least one third of the coastline is hidden beneath ice.

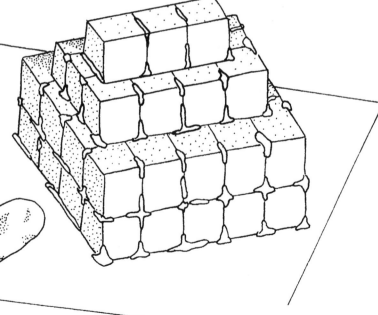

experienced   3 preparation  construction

Antarctica Snow Scene

ANTARCTICA

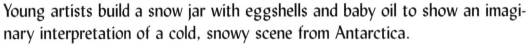

Did you know?

Antarctica is cold—very, very cold! The lowest temperature ever recorded is minus 128.6°F (-89.2¼°C) in Vostok, Antarctica on July 21, 1983. The lowest average annual temperature is minus 70°F (-56.7°C) in Plateau Station, Antarctica.

Young artists build a snow jar with eggshells and baby oil to show an imaginary interpretation of a cold, snowy scene from Antarctica.

Materials

1 hard-boiled egg
1 small jar with screw-on lid
1 small piece of green felt
pencil
scissors
glue
Styrofoam pieces
tiny evergreen branches
baby oil

Process

1. Peel the egg and set the edible part of the egg aside for a snack or meal.
2. Clean the eggshell so only the shell, not the inner coating, remains. Crush the eggshell into very fine pieces. Set aside.
3. Place the jar lid on the felt as a pattern to draw a circle on the felt. Cut the circle out of the felt. Glue the felt on the top of the jar lid.
4. Create a snowy environment on the inside bottom of the jar lid. Glue tiny Styrofoam pieces on the inside bottom of the lid to resemble areas covered with snow.
5. Glue on the small pieces of evergreen to resemble trees.
6. Let dry for ½ hour.
7. Add the crushed eggshells to the jar. Fill the jar with baby oil. Screw the jar lid on tightly.
8. Turn the jar upside down and watch the snow drift, swirl and fall over the snowy landscape.

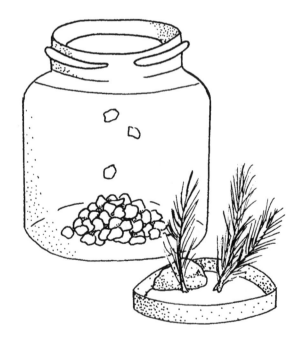

Asia

Asia is home to some of the world's oldest cultures and some of the most interesting art forms for young artists to explore. Asia's art begins in the oldest civilizations known to express themselves, from ancient architecture to tile mosaics created thousands of years ago. Stone tools were used to carve ancient works of art used in funerals and religious worship. Young artists will explore the art of ancient and modern Asia through projects such as: China Hand Made Paper, India Stone Inlay, Japan Moribana Flower Scenery, Israel Stone Mosaic, Iran No-Ruz Centerpiece, Indonesia Batik Tulis, Korea Jeweled Crown, Laos Pimia Sand Mounds, Thailand Loy Krathong Boats, and Viet Nam Tet Trung Thu Lantern. Young artists experience over 20 explorations that focus on process not product, from flower arranging to paper making, from ancient to present day art experiences.

Selected Bibliography

Cambodia

Silent Lotus by Jeanne M. Lee (Farrar, Straus & Giroux, 1991)

China

Chin Yu Min and the Ginger Cat by Jennifer Armstrong (Crown, 1993)

Dragon Kite of the Autumn Moon by Valerie Reddix (Lothrop, 1992)

The Emperor and the Kite by Jane Yolen (Putnam, 1988)

The Empty Pot by Demi (Holt, 1990)

Eyes of the Dragon by Margaret Leaf (Lothrop, 1987)

The Great Wall of China by Leonard Everett Fisher (Simon & Schuster, 1986)

Lon Po-Po: A Red Riding Hood Tale from China by Ed Young (Philomel Books, 1989)

Our Home Is the Sea by Riki Levinson (Dutton, 1988)

Seven Chinese Brothers by Margaret Mahey (Scholastic, 1990)

Tikki Tikki Tembo by Arlene Mosel (Holt, 1989)

Young Fu of the Upper Yangtze by Elizabeth Foreman Lewis (Bantam Doubleday Dell, 1990)

India

The Story of Wali Dad by Kristina Rodanas (Lothrop, 1988)

The Umbrella Thief by Sybil Wettasinghe (Kane-Miller, 1987)

Israel

The Children We Remember by Chana Byers Abells (Greenwillow, 1986)

Japan

Baseball Saved Us by Ken Mochizuki (Lee & Low, 1993)

Commodore Perry in the Land of the Shogun by Rhoda Blumberg (Lothrop, 1985)

The Crane Wife by Sumiko Yagawa (Morrow, 1987)

Hiroshima No Pika by Toshi Maruki (Lothrop, 1982)

How My Parents Learned to Eat by Ina Friedman (Houghton Mifflin, 1984)

The Stonecutter: A Japanese Folktale by Gerald McDermott (Harcourt Brace, 1995)

This Place Is Crowded by Vicki Cobb (Walker & Co., 1993)

The Two Foolish Cats by Yoshiko Uchida (Macmillan, 1987)

Korea

Korea by Karen Jacobsen (Children's Press, 1989)

Aekyung's Dream by Min Paek (Children's Press, 1988)

Philippines

Rockabye Crocodile by José Aruego and Ariane Dewey (Greenwillow, 1988)

Grandfather's Stories from the Philippines by Donna Roland and Ron Oden (Open My World, 1986)

Thailand

Thailand by Karen Jacobsen (Children's Press, 1989)

Tibet

The Mountains of Tibet by Mordicai Gerstein (HarperCollins, 1987)

Vietnam

Angel Child, Dragon Child by Maria Michele Surat (Scholastic, 1989)

Ba-Nam by Houghton Mifflin Company Staff (Houghton Mifflin, 1992)

The Brocaded Slipper and Other Vietnamese Tales by Lynette Dyer Vuong (Lippincott, 1982)

More of Grandfather's Stories from Vietnam by Donna Roland (Open My World, 1985)

Vietnam by Karen Jacobsen (Children's Press, 1992)

Eraser Signature

Young artists create simple initial stamps gouged into a large eraser, and instead of signing their art with a pencil or crayon, press the design onto an ink pad and then onto their artwork.

Materials

large pink eraser
pencil
straightened heavy paper clip or other digging tool
red ink pad (or red food coloring on a folded paper towel)
artwork

Process

1. Write the initial or initials of your name on the large pink eraser.
▲ Note: Make letters backwards so they will turn out right when printed.
2. With a heavy paper clip that has been straightened, gouge the initials into the eraser, scraping away eraser bit by bit. Other tools from around the kitchen may also work, such as a poultry skewer or the point of a knife. Adult help will be needed for sharp tools.
3. To sign and seal the artwork with the artist's initials, press the eraser into the ink of a red ink pad. Then press the inked eraser onto the corner of the artwork.
▲ Note: If an ink pad is not available, fold a paper towel into a square and dampen it with a little water. Set it on a piece of aluminum foil or a Styrofoam tray. Squeeze some red food coloring on the damp paper towel. Use this instead of an ink pad. Red tempera paint or watercolor paint will also work just fine.

CHINA

Did you know?

A Chinese artist finishes his artworks, instead of signing the work with a pencil, pen or paintbrush, by pressing his name seal on it, making a name print in red ink. Around the year 600 BC, these seals were sometimes stamped in clay tiles and prints were made from them—probably the first type of woodblock developed.

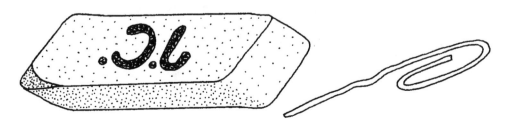

beginner   preparation   printing

Printing Press

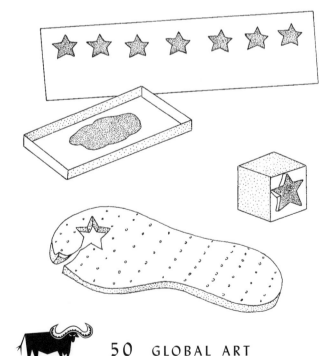

CHINA

Did you know?

China was the first country to print with paper, ink and carved wooden blocks—a process called xylography. The invention of paper in 105 AD by Ta'ai Lun provided a nice smooth, pliable surface on which to print. In this process, a single carved wooden block of words was used to print on whole pages. By the 11th century, the Chinese had cut the blocks into individual characters, creating the world's first movable type which revolutionized printing as we know it today, and a new form of communication began.

Young artists create a simple printing press from blocks of wood and a shoe insole.

Materials

soft, spongy insole from an old shoe
▲ Note: If insoles are not available, cut letters from other materials, such as

rubber inner tube	felt scrap
Styrofoam grocery tray	linoleum floor scrap
cardboard	thick balloon

pencil
scissors
block of wood or any small wood scrap
glue
red tempera paint (or any other color)
Styrofoam grocery tray
scrap paper for practice printing
paper

Process

1. Draw a letter or design on the insole or other suggested material. Draw it bold enough to be cut out with scissors, then cut.
2. Glue the letter or design on a block of wood. (Remember to glue the letter reversed or backwards so it will print right side up.)
3. Pour a puddle of red paint in a Styrofoam grocery tray.
4. Press the block into the red paint, and then press the block onto paper.
5. Continue the printing process until the desired design is completed.

Variation

Printing on white wrapping tissue makes great wrapping paper.

Ancient Stenciling

Young children explore the use of acetate for making stencils, and then sponge paint their own design on paper.

Materials

acetate (from office or graphics stores)
draftsman sticky-dots, optional (from office or graphics stores)

marker	tempera paint in saucer
scissors	paper towels
small sponge	paper

Process

1. Draw any shape, design or letter on a strip of acetate with the marker. (See the illustration.)
2. Poke a tiny hole with the scissors point to begin, then cut out the design. The cutout in the acetate becomes the stencil.
3. Place the acetate stencil on the paper, holding it still with the non-drawing hand. (If draftsman sticky-dots are available, stick them to the corners of the stencil to hold. The dots are removable and will not tear the paper or stick to the stencil.)
4. With the free hand, dip the sponge into a very small portion of paint. Dab the sponge several times on the paper towel to remove excess paint.
5. Then dab the sponge paint on the cut-out area of the stencil.
6. Let the paint dry somewhat.
7. Move the stencil to another part of the paper and repeat the dabbing process.
8. Continue moving and dabbing the stencil until satisfied with the design.

Variation

Consider making stenciled designs with appropriate types of paints or dyes on other materials such as

walls	long strips of paper	book covers
wrapping paper	fabric	table covers
greeting cards	poster borders	pillowcases

CHINA

Did you know?

Paper patterns with holes in them date back to the 10th century. For example, stencils were used to repeat an outline over and over again in The Thousand Buddha Caves in western China. This proved to be an accurate method of overlaying color and repeating identical designs in a large area.

Tangram Design Game

CHINA

Did you know?

When immigrating Chinese workers arrived in America, they brought an interesting puzzle game with them. This game, called a tangram, consisted of seven wooden pieces—five triangles, one square and one rhomboid. The object of the game was to put the pieces together to make designs or pictures.

Young artists construct the seven shapes of the traditional tangram and then make designs or patterns with the shapes.

Materials

pencil
heavy paper or cardboard
ruler
scissors

Process

1. Draw a large square on a sheet of heavy paper or cardboard. The square should measure 9″ x 9″ (23 cm x 23 cm).
2. Use the ruler to divide the square into triangles, one square and one rhomboid, as shown in the illustration. Or, enlarge the illustration and trace the patterns for the five shapes shown.
3. Cut them out of the paper.
4. Explore and manipulate the shapes, making different designs and pictures.

Variations

✓ Trace the *outline only* of a pattern made with the tangram pieces on a sheet of paper. Remove the pieces. Have a friend try to fit the pieces back into the pattern outline.
✓ Follow the first variation, but use only triangles. Leave the other pieces out.

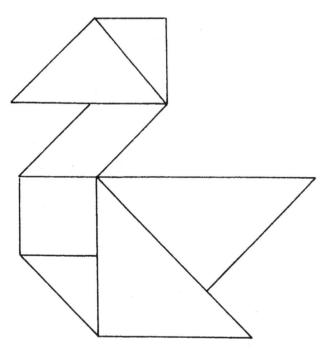

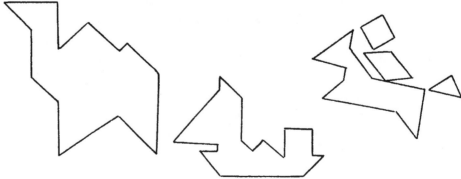

Handmade Paper

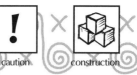
Young artists blend scrap paper with grasses or flower petals and water, then press the pulp onto a screen, creating a lovely sheet of art paper.

Materials

white scrap paper
blender (with adult supervision) and water
pine needles, leaves (broken into tiny pieces), flower petals, blades of grass
pan and 2 screens
old towel and newspapers
can
pressing cloth
heavy book
iron, optional

Process

1. Tear the scrap paper into small pieces and put them into the blender so it is half full.
2. Fill the blender with enough water to make it three-fourths full. Turn the blender on medium speed until the paper is blended into a pulp.
3. Add the pine needles, leaves and other small materials to the pulp. Blend for one or two seconds more.
4. Place a screen over the pan. Pour the watery pulp over the screen, spreading the pulp out in a square shape. Let the water drain off into the pan for 30 minutes.
5. To drain the water from the pulp further, put an old towel on top of a stack of newspapers. Carefully lift the pulp covered screen and put it on the towel. Put another piece of screen on top of the pulp and roll the water out with the can. This can be done by rolling the can with the palm of the hand.
6. Lift the screen, then flip it over onto the pressing cloth. Peel the screen off the set paper very carefully.
7. Fold the pressing cloth over the wet paper and press until almost dry.
8. Put a heavy book on it overnight to flatten. Iron to flatten and help dry, if desired.
▲ Note: The dry paper will be a pretty art paper to look at, but too thick and soft for every-day letter writing or picture drawing.

CHINA

Did you know?

Paper was invented by Ta'ai Lun in 105 AD. An endless variety of materials such as vegetable fiber, rags, old paper, bamboo, straw, wood and other materials can be shredded, crushed and mixed with glue to become a pulp, made eventually into paper. China's paper making formula was kept secret for many centuries until war broke out with the Arabs. The paper makers were captured and ordered by the Arab soldiers to reveal their paper-making secrets. Their method of making paper then spread throughout the world.

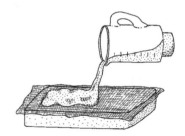

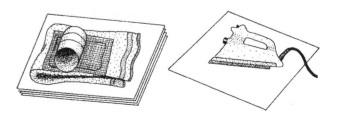

Story Banner

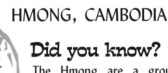

HMONG, CAMBODIA

Did you know?

The Hmong are a group of Cambodian nomadic people who originated in China, Burma and Laos. The Hmong make banners that tell stories of everyday Hmong life or beloved Hmong legends. The art technique can be very complicated, combining sewing, embroidering and batik.

Young artists make a simplified version of the Hmong banner by tracing shapes from a story drawing onto fabric and then attaching the cut-out shapes to a large piece of fabric for the banner.

Materials

newspaper or newsprint
markers, pencils, crayons
scissors
tape
fabric or felt scraps and fabric banner, about 12" x 14' (30 cm x 4 m)
fabric glue
needle, thread and embroidery floss, optional

Process

1. On the newspaper or newsprint draw a story with large, simple shapes. Draw about something real or something imaginary.
2. Cut out the largest shapes.
3. Tape each of these shapes on a fabric scrap or felt square in a color that goes well with the shapes. Trace the shapes with a marker. Then remove the tape.
4. Cut out the shapes with scissors. Place the shapes on the larger piece of fabric or banner in a design or in an order that helps tell a story.
5. Tape the shapes in place. Glue or sew them onto the fabric banner. If glued, dry overnight.
6. Write words on the banner with markers to help tell the story, if desired. Embroider over the words and letters, if desired.
7. Hang the banner to enjoy the design and story. Tell a story out loud about the shapes on the banner.

Diwali Alpanas

Young artists cut stencils from butcher paper and make stencil patterns on the ground outdoors with colored sand.

Materials

large squares of butcher paper
good sharp scissors
bag of sand, powdered tempera and newspaper to make colored sand (see directions)
box or tray

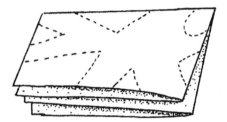

Process

1. Fold the large square of butcher paper in half, and then in half again.
2. Cut a lacy design like a big snowflake from the folds and edges in the paper. The holes should be big and open. The leftover paper design should be bold.
3. Unfold the stencil.
4. Select a walkway or area outdoors on a calm day. Place the stencil flat on the ground. Pour some of the colored sand into the different spaces and holes in the stencil. Then carefully lift the stencil, trying not to drop sand on the design. This part usually needs adult help.
5. Pour the extra sand into a box or tray to use again.
6. Move the stencil over next to the design, and repeat the process. Use some of the extra sand from the tray too.
7. Continue stenciling with the sand until satisfied with the design. Sometimes, if enough people help, the stenciling can line an entire sidewalk!
8. The next day, sweep up the leftover sand and discard or mix into a garden.

To color sand: For each color, spread a section of newspapers on the floor. Pour some sand into the center of each section of papers. Mix a different color of powdered tempera paint into each sand pile with a stick or with hands to a desired shade. Let the sand piles dry, if moist. Pour the colored sand back into buckets or other containers. (Purchased sand is cleaner and nicer, but beach sand works fine too, although it tends to be a little smelly.)

INDIA

Did you know?

Diwali, the Festival of Lights, marks the beginning of the Hindu new year in India, usually in October or November. Buildings were traditionally illuminated with oil-burning bowls called dipa lights and today are often lighted with strings of electric lights. Houses are whitewashed, old debts paid off, new clothes purchased and homes thoroughly cleaned. Good luck designs called "alpana" are created on steps, porches, in doorways and on walkways with paper stencils and a mixture of rice flour and colored powders.

beginner   preparation   painting

Kathakali Face Painting

INDIA

Did you know?

Kathakali performances are story-plays that mix dance and drama. These plays originated on the southwest coast of India as a unique type of theater based on centuries old myths and legends. The face paint in the Kathakali theater is important and elaborate because it is the only costume the character wears. Otherwise, the performer wears everyday clothing.

Young artists paint their faces in the style of the Kathakali theater performers and may choose to put on a play while dressed in face paint costumes.

Materials

liquid tempera paints (add hand lotion or cold cream to the paints for easy face clean up)
painting tools, such as
    paintbrushes with different points and sizes, cotton swabs, cotton balls
paper towels and facial tissues, soap and water, for clean up

Process

Faces can be painted in any design or for any character. The following directions represent one choice for a face paint design that is striking and bold like a clown-face, typical of Kathakali-style face painting as shown in the illustration. Other original face paintings are also encouraged.

1. Paint a dark colored line from one ear down around the chin to the other ear to resemble a beard.
2. Carefully, paint large sweeping lines around the eyes in another bright color.
3. Put two black marks in the middle of the forehead like a wrinkled brow.
4. Paint the lips red and on each side of the mouth put two red circles.
5. Add two upside down joined triangles at the top of the forehead in orange. Color around the triangles and the two black dots with yellow.
6. Put a white dot on the end of the nose.
7. Fill in all of the uncolored areas of the face with green.
8. Put on a play dressed in face paint costume!

Other face-painting ideas
storybook characters
clowns
outer space aliens
animals or creatures—lion, tiger, bear, elephant, spider, snake, insects
pets—dog, cat, fish, mouse
family members—baby, sibling, grandparent, parent

Stone Inlay

Young artists place hobby gemstones and multicolored pebbles in a self-hardening clay base to imitate the stone inlays of India.

Materials

self-hardening clay
multicolored pebbles
hobby gemstones

Process

1. Mold the clay into a box shape. Make a clay lid for the box too. The box can be round, square, rectangular or even triangular.
2. When the box is complete but while the clay is still moist, gently press the stones and gems into the clay, making designs and patterns.
3. Let the clay dry thoroughly.

INDIA

Did you know?

India is known for the art of beautiful stone inlay. Artisans make designs by cutting semiprecious stones and then setting them in marble or soapstone.

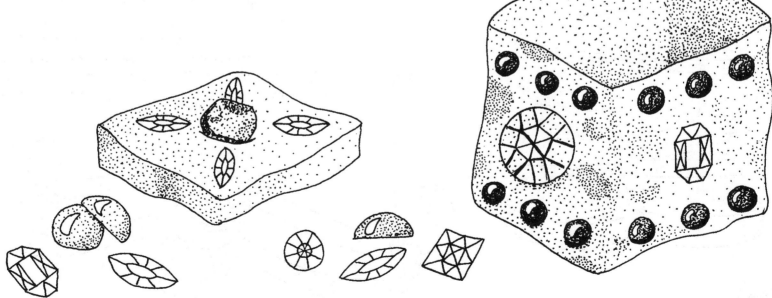

No-Ruz Centerpiece

IRAN

Did you know?

In Iran the new year celebration, No-Ruz, begins on the first day of spring and lasts for twelve days. Families place a damp piece of cloth in a bowl and sprinkle it with lentil or wheat seeds, which then grow into a lush, green centerpiece for the holiday table. On the last day of No-Ruz, families picnic near a stream, after which they toss the bowl of greenery into the running stream to symbolize throwing away unhappy times from the old year.

The young artist uses lentil seeds to grow a bowl of greenery in an aluminum pie plate for No-Ruz. A small box is covered with collage magazine clippings for a display stand.

Materials

To grow the lentils

aluminum pie plate, damp cloth or paper towels and water
lentil seeds or other edible seeds, such as
    wheat, alfalfa, soy bean, chickpea

To create the display box

cardboard cigar box or school box
scissors and magazine pictures
white glue in a dish and paintbrush
newspaper-covered work area

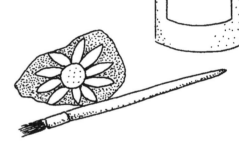

Process

Growing the lentils

1. About a week before No-Ruz (or anytime), place a damp rag, cloth or paper towels in the aluminum pie plate. Choose a cloth that fits the plate.
2. Sprinkle the cloth with lentil seeds (or seeds of other grains, beans or peas). Place on a shelf or table, but not in hot sunlight. Keep the cloth moist for the next several days and the seeds will sprout into a lush, green pan full of sprouts.

Creating the display box

1. Place the cardboard school box on the newspapers, upside down.
2. Clip magazine pictures from an old magazine. Pictures of springtime gardens and flowers are nice, but any pictures and colors will do. Begin painting the magazine pictures on the box with white glue and a paintbrush, covering all the edges of each picture. Overlap the pictures as more and more are added. Cover the bottom and sides of the box. Dry.
3. Turn the box over and finish covering the top of the box too. Then dry overnight.
4. Place the box on the table and use to display the green centerpiece.

Cylinder Seal

Young artists make a seal with a rolling pin and playdough, similar in use to that of the King of Ur.

Materials

cardboard
markers, pencils or crayons
scissors
old wooden rolling pin
tacky glue
playdough
objects to press into the playdough, such as
    buttons
    pieces of toys
    kitchen tools
    fingertips

Process

1. Draw a symbol, letter or simple shape on the cardboard and cut it out. Draw as many symbols as desired and cut those out too.
2. Glue the symbols on the old rolling pin with tacky glue. Let the glue dry several hours or overnight.
3. Pat and flatten out some playdough on the work surface.
4. Roll the rolling pin with all its shapes over the playdough and see impressions made from the cardboard shapes and symbols appear in the playdough.
5. Experiment with pressing other things into the dough to see what impressions they will make.
6. Create a message on a slab of play-dough and deliver it to someone important, complete with an "official" seal of royalty pressed into the dough!

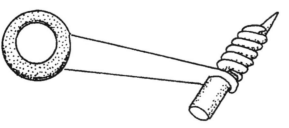

IRAQ

Did you know?

When the King of the ancient country of Ur (today known as Iraq) sent a message to far away places or when he made a new law, he stamped his royal seal on the clay tablet document to make it official. The royal seal was made of stone and contained carved scenes of the king's life or symbols for his name. When people saw the clay tablet with the royal seal, they knew the message was officially from the King of Ur.

some experience   preparation   construction

Silverware Bells

ISRAEL

Did you know?

Bells were used in many ancient civilizations. In the 10th century BC, King Solomon installed large gold bells on the roof of his royal home to frighten away the birds.

Young artists create bells (wind chimes) from old silverware that make beautiful sounds.

Materials

old silverware
string
scissors
bar, stick or pipe to hang the silverware from, such as a
    clothes hanger
    stick
    wood dowel
    tree branch
    metal pipe
    broom handle

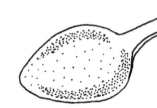

Process

1. Collect old silverware from garage sales or thrift shops.
2. Tie a varying length of string to each selected piece of silverware. Six to ten pieces work well, but use no less than three.
3. Tie the loose end of the string to the hanger or stick, arranging the strings so that when the silverware swings or moves, the pieces clang into one another.
4. Hang the silverware wind chimes in the wind. Listen to the beautiful bells like King Solomon's in ancient Israel.

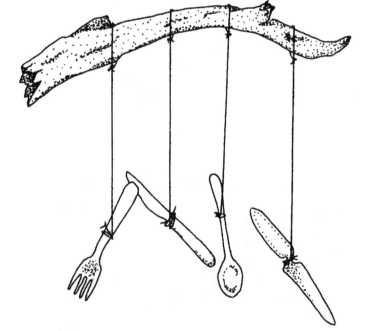

Stone Mosaic

sculpture   preparation **3**   experienced

Young artists make a stone mosaic design with pebbles collected from a walk outdoors pressed directly into wet grout in a sturdy box.

Materials

sturdy box or tray, lined with aluminum foil (boxes or trays with sharp corners make a nice-looking finished work)

grout for tile, available from a hardware store

mixing container, such as an old plastic bowl or small bucket

water and stick for stirring

piece of board or old 6" (15 cm) ruler

pebbles of every color, collected from a walk (flattened lentil-shaped stones are nice, but any pebbles are fine)

newspaper-covered work area

Process

1. Line a box or tray with aluminum foil.
2. Mix the tile grout with water in an old container to a thick, creamy consistency, following the directions on the box to make cement.
   ▲ Note: Do not rinse any of this material down the drain or a serious clog may occur.
3. Pour the cement into the bottom of the box to about ¼"–½" (6–13 mm) thick. Smooth the cement with the edge of a board or an old 6" ruler.
4. While the cement is still wet, press stones into it one at a time creating a design. Begin setting stones in the middle of the cement first and near the edges last.
5. Dry for two or three days, but not in the sun. Drying cannot be rushed.
6. Gently turn the box upside down on a pad of newspapers and allow to dry further if necessary. Pull away the aluminum foil.
7. Turn the mosaic design over and see the design. Use the mosaic as an outdoor garden decoration or for decorative enjoyment anywhere.

ISRAEL

Did you know?

Mosaics are one of the oldest forms of art. The earliest discoveries date from the 4th century BC. Mosaics were made of shells and stones showing designs of warriors, cattle, a banquet and even a checkerboard game.

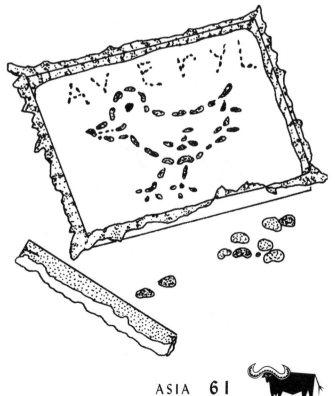

Gyotaku Art

JAPAN

★ Did you know?

"The fish I caught was thiiiiiis big!" Everyone has a fish tale to tell, but how do you know how big the fish really was? In Japan, the ancient art of taking prints from fish was called gyotaku and was developed in the 1800's to accurately document fish size. A fish is inked, then paper is pressed onto it to make a print (gyo - fish; taku - impression).

This activity is a good way for young artists to mesh science and math with art in designing the composition of the gyotaku print while learning about how fish really look and measuring their sizes.

Materials

newspapers
fresh fish
water, soap, paper towels
sand or salt, optional
clay
straight pins, optional
tempera paint in different colors in aluminum pie tins
paintbrushes, at least two
paper for printing, such as
    construction paper
    newsprint
    paper towel
    rice paper
▲ Note: Rice paper should be available through art or stationary stores or in shops that sell Japanese calligraphy materials.

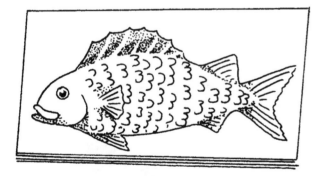

Process

1. Cover the work area with newspapers.
2. Wipe the fish thoroughly of any excess moisture and place it on a thick pad of newspaper. It might help to rub the fish with some salt or sand and then rinse it. Pat dry.
3. Fan out the fins into an open position and arrange the fish in a pleasing position. As an optional process, lumps of clay or small wads of paper towels can be placed under the fins and tail to spread them open and support them upwards. Pins can be placed on the under-side of the fins and tail to keep them open. Small bits of clay/paper towel pieces can also be placed under the gill cover and in the mouth to hold these parts open. If fish has been gutted, stuff with crumpled newspaper to keep its shape.
4. Paint one side of the fish with different colors of paint, painting the entire fish. Apply the paint or ink directly onto the fish, avoiding the eye area. If the paint is applied too thickly, some features may be obscured. On a large scaled fish, try brushing from tail to head (against the scales) to get more details. Work quickly so paint doesn't dry.
5. Gently and carefully place a sheet of paper over the fish, starting with the center of the fish. Firmly press it into the contours of the fish to make the print, but be gentle with the fins and tail.
6. Carefully lift the paper off the fish so that the print does not smudge. Let the paint dry thoroughly.
7. One fish can be used to print several times. Just wash it off and repaint.

▲ Note: To avoid waste, you can use a rubber fish such as the one available from Nasco (1-800-558-9595).

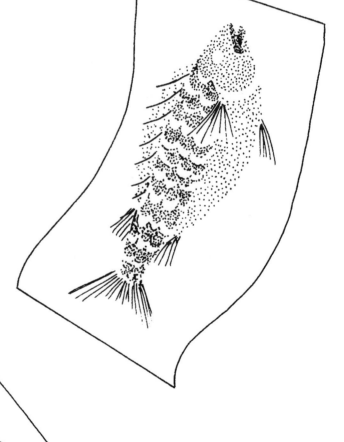

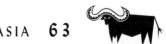

Karensansui Mini-Garden

JAPAN

Did you know?

During the Kamakura period, from 1185-1333, Zen Buddhism arrived in Japan from China, influencing Japanese spiritual life and soon extending its influence to Japanese gardens. Zen gardens were designed for contemplation and meditation. The Karensansui (dry landscape) approach to gardens used stones to represent mountains and raked sand to suggest flowing, moving water.

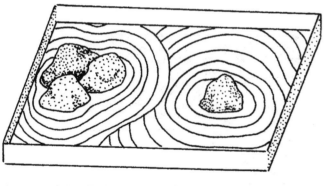

Young artists create a miniature Karensansui garden in a large, shallow pan with rocks for mountains and sand for water.

Materials

large, shallow baking pan or cookie sheet with edges
moist sand
pebbles or small rocks
cardboard rectangles about the size of combs
scissors
misting water bottle, optional

Process

1. Fill a large, shallow baking pan or cookie sheet with clean sand. Be sure the cookie sheet or pan has edges.
2. The sand should be moist. (Water can be misted or sprinkled over the sand to moisten, if necessary.) Pat the sand into the pan.
3. Arrange several pebbles in the sand to symbolize a few mountains surrounded by water.
4. Cut some spaces in the edge of the cardboard rectangle to look like a comb with widely spaced teeth.
5. Comb the sand to make designs that look like ripples of water. Experiment and explore with the sand designs. Pat down designs and try new ones. The sand should look like flowing, moving water when done.
6. Place the Zen Karensansui garden on a table or window ledge and contemplate its landscape. (Contemplate means to look at, study and think deeply about what is seen and what it might mean.) If you look at the Karensansui garden long enough, the rocks really do begin to look like mountains surrounded by actual moving water.
7. The garden can be changed at any time to arrange new mountains and water or simply to tidy up the landscape with fresh raking of sand.

Kai-awase Shells

Young artists design matching sets of clam shells with permanent markers and then play a simplified version of Kai-awase with a friend.

Materials

oatmeal container
construction paper and colored markers
scissors
glue or tape
soap, water and towel
clam or scallop shells, see options
fine-tipped permanent markers

Process

1. Measure enough construction paper to cover the oatmeal container. Trim away excess paper.
2. Decorate the construction paper that will wrap around the container with markers. Cover the cardboard oatmeal container with the decorated construction paper. Secure it with tape or glue. Set aside.
3. Wash each shell, if needed, and dry with a towel.
▲ Option: If clam shells or scallop shells are not available, draw a fist-sized shell on a piece of paper. Cut this out and use it for a pattern to trace shells on white cardboard or matte board. Cut these out and use for the shells.
4. On the inside of each shell draw a scene or picture with the fine-tip permanent markers. Then draw a matching shell. All the shell drawings should be done in pairs.
5. Play Kai-awase with several friends. Pour all the shells out on a carpeted floor or other soft surface. Turn them all face down. Next take turns turning a shell face up, looking at the picture inside and then turning another shell face up, trying to match the pictures. If they don't match, it is the other player's turn.
6. When a match is made, tell a little imaginary story about what is happening in the shell picture, or a short poem or song could also be made up about each matching shell design. When finished playing, place all the shells in the cardboard container for storage.

JAPAN

Did you know?

Kai-awase originated in the 12th century as a shell game for children of the rich and has since developed into an intricate art form. The shells look alike when face down, but when turned over, tiny scenes of Japanese life or scenes of good fortune are delicately painted on the insides. The object of the game is to turn over two matching shells, then recite a poem about the scene or describe its theme. The child with the most matches wins.

some experience

1
preparation

construction

Moribana Flower Scenery

JAPAN

★ Did you know?

Japanese flower arranging is a creative art hundreds of years old. Moribana, one of the styles of flower arrangement in Japan, is translated as "piled-up or clustered flowers" and uses a low open-mouthed bowl or container. Moribana draws on imagination but is easy to make. The main idea of Moribana scenery style flower arranging is to depict a miniature version of a woodland scene with a stream or small pond.

Young children create a miniature woodland scene with collected branches, plants, leaves and bark placed in a low container. The pond can be made from a mirror or aluminum foil partially buried in the soil.

Materials

newspaper covered work area
low, open bowl or container (a baking pan works well)
soil
collection of living, artificial or dry materials for flower arranging, such as

branches	plants
flowers	bark
leaves	grasses

gravel or pebbles
small mirror or aluminum foil
little statue, toy or figurine, optional

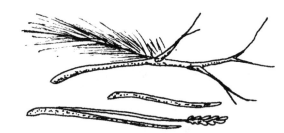

Process

1. Fill the low container with a layer of soil about 1–2" (3–5 cm) deep. Pat smooth and flat.
2. Look at the container and think about a woodland scene to design. Think about paths, ponds, trees, stones and how to arrange things to look like real trees and plants. For example, stand a small branch into the soil to represent a tree, plant some clover to look like bushes, stand some grass to look like reeds along a stream. Use imagination.
3. Add pebbles or gravel to represent rocks or boulders.
4. Bury the edges of a cosmetic mirror or a piece of aluminum foil to represent a pond or stream.
5. Once the Moribana looks like a real woodland scene in miniature, the work is done. Sometimes adding a little statue, toy or figurine helps the miniature scale of the Moribana look more realistic.

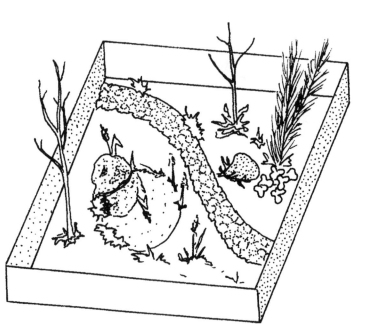

Batik Tulis

Young children explore a simplified batik tulis method using a flour and water paste instead of wax and dye. The results are beautiful and give the artist a feel for the batik process, but save about three days to complete this two-color project.

Materials

To begin the batik
small piece of 100% white cotton or muslin fabric, unlaundered
tape
heavy cardboard
½ cup (70 g) flour and ½ cup (125 ml) water
2 teaspoons (10 ml) alum from the spice shelf at a grocery story
blender
squeeze bottle, one for each artist

To dye the batik
2 paste food colors, from cake decorating department
at least two shallow, clean tuna cans, one for each color
water
paintbrushes

Process

Traditionally, to make batik, hot wax is applied to a smooth cloth with a canting, a pen-like tool that holds liquid wax. When the wax is cold, the cloth is immersed in a bath of dye which colors only the unwaxed parts of the fabric. Wax is then added to protect previously dyed areas or scraped off to expose new areas to accept dye. The process is repeated as many times as desired, using darker and darker colors each time until the final color is reached. Finally, all wax is scraped off and the fabric is boiled to remove any trace of wax. This traditional form of batik is a difficult, time-consuming and intricate art form.

JAVA, INDONESIA

Did you know?

The people of Java, one of the islands of Indonesia, are world famous as batik artists and were making batik cloth as early as the 12th century. The word batik means "to dot" in Javanese. "Batik tulis" means "written batik" because the patterns are drawn on the fabric in a freehand style.

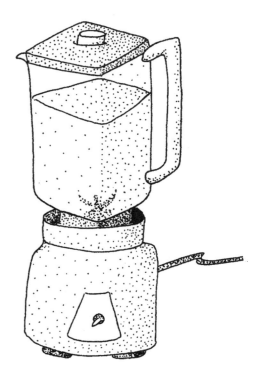

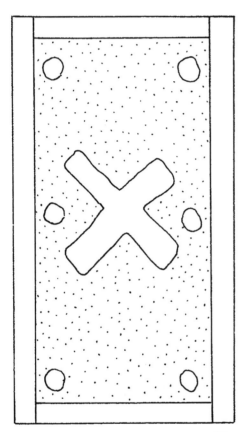

1. Tape the muslin square to a piece of cardboard. Tape all around the edges like a picture frame, keeping the fabric fairly smooth and unwrinkled. Set aside.
2. With adult help, mix the flour, water and alum into a paste in the blender. Then put the paste into a squeeze bottle. Draw with the paste on the muslin. Dots, lines and solids are effective. Then dry overnight. (Seal the paste bottle tightly for using again tomorrow.)
3. The next day, mix a light color of paste food coloring such as yellow or light shades of green, pink or blue, in a shallow tuna can with some water. Then paint over the dry paste design. Dry completely again, perhaps overnight.
4. When the color is dry, chip and rub the dry paste off the muslin with fingers.
5. Draw another paste design over the light color design. Dry overnight.
6. The next day, mix a darker or deeper can of paste food coloring that will complement the lighter shade. Paint over the dry paste design. Dry again, probably overnight.
7. When the second layer of color is dry, chip and rub the dry paste off the muslin again.
▲ Note on layering and adding colors: Many layers of colors can be added to this beginning two-layer project; it will just take additional days of drying. The artist can decide how far to go with the layering of colors and paste, but it is not necessary to stop with two colors.
8. Remove the tape from the fabric, and the batik is complete, or keep the batik on the cardboard for display.
▲ Note: The batik could also be attached to a folded piece of heavy paper as a greeting card, framed or sewn to a larger piece of fabric. For a group project or an energetic single artist, a larger piece of fabric can be batiked.

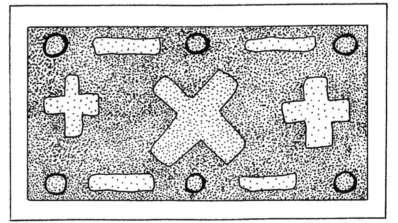

Jeweled Crown

Young artists design crowns festooned with hobby jewels and sewing trims.

Materials

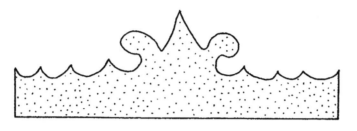

string

scissors

heavy paper head band

sheet of heavy paper

pencil

crown decorations such as

    felt scraps; hobby jewels and gems; ribbons, cords, yarn, embroidery floss;

    gold and silver rickrack and sewing trims; glitter and sequins; beads, buttons, feathers

stapler

glue

Process

1. To measure the crown to fit, with adult help wrap a piece of string around the head of the person who will wear the crown. Hold the measured mark with fingers. Then remove the string, and cut it at the mark.
2. Stretch the string on the heavy paper head band and mark the length. Add a few more inches (or centimeters) to the headband for an overlap, and then cut away the extra. Set aside.
3. Double a heavy sheet of paper. On the doubled sheet of heavy paper, draw points, swirls or other shapes for the decorative part of the crown. Cut this out.
4. Staple the double-thick crown design to the head band. Use enough staples to make the crown secure.
5. Choose from a collection of art materials and scraps to decorate the crown. Glue on hobby jewels and gems, glitter, ribbons, felt shapes, feathers, sewing trims, rickrack and so on. Make the crown very elaborate, glittery and fancy. Then let the crown dry overnight until it is hard and strong.
6. Bring the two ends of the headband together, checking to see if the crown fits, and then staple. Wear the elaborately decorated crown.
▲ Note: If the crown is too heavy from all the decorating and won't stand up straight, add another layer of heavy paper to the inside of the crown to help keep it firm and strong.

KOREA

Did you know?

Korea is a mountainous peninsula about the size of Utah projecting south from the eastern Asian mainland, the historic land bridge between China and Japan. Korean skills in metal-craft can be traced to about 1000 BC. Korea incorporated its rich history and skill of metal art as part of its royalty's attire. Korean kings of long ago wore elaborately decorated metal crowns, each carefully designed and artfully created, containing countless jewels and precious stones.

Pimia Sand Mounds

LAOS

Did you know?

Pimia is the celebration of the Laotian New Year. It is during spring and lasts for 3 days. People go to the temples and make mounds of sand in the courtyards which will be used later to make repairs to the temples. But on Pimia, the sand mounds are decorated with flowers, money, toys and flags. Pimia also includes water throwing and feasting. Pimia is a happy celebration with much laughing and playing.

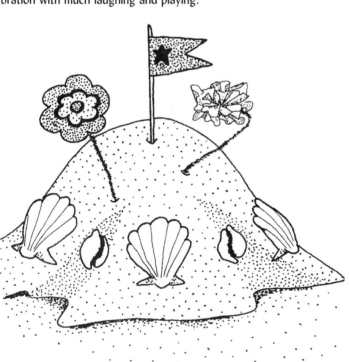

Young artists make mounds of sand outside in a sandbox or inside in a sand table. The mounds are then decorated with handmade flags, play money, paper flowers or other choices of special things.

Materials

outdoor area such as a sandbox, or an indoor sand table
sand
art materials and collectibles for decorating the sand, such as

paper scraps	bamboo skewers	tape	pipe cleaners
pine cones	grasses or weeds	shells	toys

Process

1. Make a nice mound of sand in the sandbox or sand table. Any size is fine.
2. Decorate the sand with anything of choice, such as
   - ✓ paper flags with scraps of paper taped to bamboo skewers (supervise closely)
   - ✓ paper flower made with art tissue and pipe cleaners
   - ✓ little toys placed in patterns and designs around the sand
   - ✓ grasses or weeds pushed into the sand
   - ✓ shells, pine cones or other natural items arranged in the sand
   - ✓ streamers cut from paper and draped on the sand
   - ✓ created paper money sprinkled around the sand
3. Create as many sand mounds as desired to enjoy the celebration of Pimia.

Loy Krathong Boats

Young artists build boats from scraps, junk, flowers and leaves which they then float in a wading pool or water table.

Materials

For the base of the floating boat, choose one

Styrofoam sandwich container

clear plastic salad bar container

aluminum foil

scraps of wood

small cardboard boxes

To decorate the boat

fabric scraps

paper scraps

sewing trims and ribbons

nuts and pennies

birthday candles

plastic or metal lids

flowers, leaves

clay

hammer, nails, tacks, stapler, glue, string, rubber bands, paper clips, etc.

For the water

water table, wading pool or real pond

matches, with adult assistance, optional

Process

1. Provide a variety of scraps and materials for boat building.
2. Attach in any way bits and pieces of materials to a base, such as a block of wood or a Styrofoam sandwich container.
3. Add real flowers and leaves.
4. Add nuts (be careful of children with allergies to nuts) and pennies as symbols of good luck and fortune.
5. Top off the boat with a birthday candle for show. Secure with a bit of clay.
6. Float the boat in a water table, wading pool or with adult assistance in a real pond!

Lighting Candles

Light candles only with adult assistance during the floating and only if candles are checked by adults to be secure and then blown out before the boats are removed from the water. Enjoy the lighted boats in a darkened room or at night.

THAILAND

Did you know?

Loy Krathong is a traditional Thai festival celebrating water and its bounty. Loy Krathong takes place just before harvest time in mid-November on a night with a full moon. Thais meet on the banks of rivers and canals to float boats which are made of cardboard, plastic and wood, elaborately decorated with flowers and leaves and illuminated with candles. The boats often contain offerings such as money or nuts to make up for wrong doings of the past year.

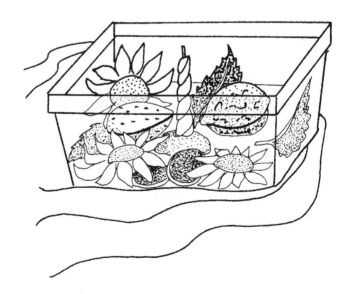

Tet Trung Thu Lantern

VIETNAM

Did you know?

Tet Trung Thu is a mid-autumn festival held to honor the beauty of the moon on the 15th day of the 8th month of the Chinese lunar calendar. Moon cakes are eaten and given as gifts, and children create lanterns in the shapes of animals or other objects. After dark, children place candles in their lanterns and parade through the streets to the crashing of cymbals and the beating of drums.

Each young artist creates a paper lantern from a construction paper tube and then hangs it from a sturdy dowel.

Materials

construction paper rectangle approximately 8" x 14" (20 cm x 35 cm)
small paper plate for the base
scissors, tape and glue
colorful art tissue paper
hole punch
string
dowel
glow-stick or small flashlight

Process

1. Measure a piece of construction paper about 8" (20 cm) tall, and long enough to go around the diameter of the paper plate. (See illustration.) Trim the rectangle to form a cylinder that will be the paper lantern.
2. Cut shapes from the construction paper, such as moons and stars, geometric shapes, animal shapes or other designs. Do not cut near the edges of the rectangle, only the center areas.
3. Cut pieces of tissue paper and tape or glue them on the back of the construction paper to cover the holes. Use as many colors as desired.
4. Roll the construction paper into a cylinder and tape the long edge. Next tape it to the paper plate base.
5. With a hole punch, go around the top edge of the lantern and make four holes, spacing them evenly around the lantern.
6. Tie an equal length of string through each of the holes. Gather the four strings above the lantern and tie them to the dowel.
7. Place a glow-stick (from camping or hardware stores) or a small flashlight in the lantern. Have a lantern parade in the evening or in a darkened room. Add noisy cymbals and loud drums to complete the celebration of the moon.

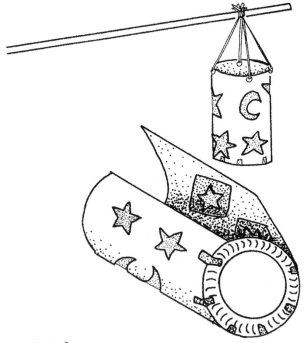

Europe

The arts, inventions and celebrations of Europe offer children an opportunity to explore the past, from ancient Roman and Greek times, through the modern world of today. Young artists express the variety of European cultures through such projects as Czechoslovakia Crayon Eggs, France Silhouettes, Germany Beeswax Modeling, Britain Button Pearlies, Greece Bread Dough Coins, Italy Roman Mosaics, Netherlands Shell Decorating, Norway Rose Maling, Poland Simple Transparencies, Russia Jeweled Eggs, Scotland Kaleidoscope, Spain Salsa Rosa Necklace, Sweden Straw Ornaments and Switzerland Egg Dye. Over 25 projects from jewelry to architecture will fascinate young artists.

Selected Bibliography

Eastern Europe

Elinda Who Danced in the Sky by Lynn Maroney (Children's Press, 1990)

It Could Always Be Worse: A Yiddish Folk Tale by Margot Zemach (Farrar, Straus & Giroux, 1990)

Mazel and Shlimaze, or Milk of a Lioness by Isaac Bashevish Singer (Farrar, Straus & Giroux, 1967)

England

Go Away, Bad Dreams by Susan Hill (Random House, 1985)

Finland

Louhi, Witch of North Farm by Toni DeGerez (Viking, 1986)

France

The Beast of Monsieur Racine by Tomi Ungerer (Farrar, Straus & Giroux, 1971)

The Glorious Flight: Across the Channel with Louis Bleriot by Alice and Martin Provensen (Viking, 1983)

Madeline by Ludwig Bemelmans (Viking, 1993)

The Red Balloon by Albert LaMorisse (Doubleday, 1967)

Stone Soup by Marcia Brown (Simon & Schuster, 1947)

Italy

Rome Antics by David Macauley (Houghton Mifflin, 1997)

Ireland

Daniel O'Rourke by Gerald McDermott (Viking, 1986)

Norway

Boy: Tales of Childhood by Roald Dahl (Farrar, Straus & Giroux, 1984)

Russia

Annie...Anya: A Month in Moscow by Irene Trivas (Orchard, 1992)

Babushka: An Old Russian Folktale by Charles Mikolaycak (Holiday, 1984)

Babushka's Mother Goose by Patricia Polacco (Putnam, 1995)

It Happened In Pinsk by Arthur Yorinks (Farrar, Straus & Giroux, 1983)

Little Sister and the Month Brothers by Beatrice S. De Regniers (Houghton Mifflin, 1976)

Peter and the Wolf by Sergei Prokofiev (Puffin, 1986)

Uncle Vova's Tree by Patricia Polacco (Putnam, 1989)

Sweden

The Tomten and the Fox by Astrid Lindgren (Putnam, 1989)

Wales

The Selkie Girl by Susan Cooper (Simon & Schuster, 1986)

Wedding Chair

Young artists paint a special chair to celebrate a chosen special event—even a wedding!

Materials

brown paper (old grocery sack or mailing paper)
pencil
crayons
old chair with flat surface on the backrest
acrylic non-toxic paints in bright colors such as
　　blue, black, white, green, red
paintbrushes
water
plastic varnish (or any clear hobby coating) and paintbrush

Process

1. Think of a special event to celebrate—possibly even a wedding. Any special event will do, such as a birthday, a holiday, the birth of a baby sister, welcome to a new pet and so on.
2. Draw the design on brown paper with a pencil.
3. Color the design with crayons. This will be the pattern to follow.
4. Draw the same pattern on the backrest of the chair with the pencil. Paint the design with acrylic paints.
5. When complete, rinse brushes in water and wipe dry.
6. Allow the chair to dry overnight or longer. Then, with adult help, paint over the painted design with plastic varnish to protect.

AUSTRIA

Did you know?

In Austria, a wedding calls for a specially painted chair called the Hockzeitsstufh, or wedding chair. Wedding scenes featuring the bride and groom, musicians, wedding party members or dancers in the festivity are painted on the back of the chair to record the blissful event and also to decorate a lasting memento for the wedding couple.

beginner   preparation   drawing

 **Crayon Eggs**

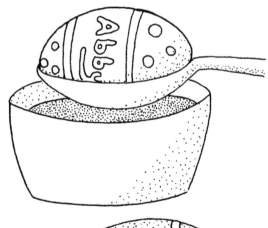

CZECHOSLOVAKIA

Did you know?

Czechoslovakian people are widely known for their lavishly detailed, hand-painted Easter eggs. Their egg designs make use of symbols and shapes that are meaningful to the individual artist.

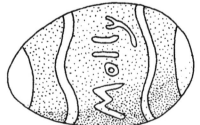

Young artists decorate eggs (for Easter or any other time) using common seasonal egg dye and wax crayons, incorporating favorite symbols of spring or other individual ideas.

Materials

egg dye	hard-boiled eggs
cups	wax crayons
vinegar	spoon
crepe paper, optional	egg holder

Process

1. Mix the egg dye according to package directions. Put each color of dye in a cup, adding a little vinegar to set the color. (Optional dye: Place crepe paper in water in a cup. When the color is strong, discard the paper. Add a little vinegar to set the color.)

2. Draw a design on a cool hard-boiled egg with wax crayons. Color firmly but gently. Some ideas for symbols and designs might be

Symbols

bunny	chick	duck	flower
cross	sunshine	child's name	heart

Designs

scallops	zigzags	wiggles	squares
polka dots	plaid	curlicues	loops

3. Lower the egg into a cup of dye with a spoon. Roll the egg around in the dye to coat all sides with the dye. Watch the color resist the crayon marks.

▲ Note: Some artists like to dip the egg in more than one color. One way is to dip the egg partially in one color and then move to a second or third color for a variety effect. Other artists like to dip the entire egg in more than one color to see how the colors mix.

4. Remove the egg from the dye when the color is strong and place on the egg holder to dry.

Button Pearlies

! caution ⬛ construction 2 preparation ★★ some experience

Young artists decorate clothing with white buttons. Although simple designs are great, flamboyant ones are fun—just like the Pearlies of London.

Materials

old piece of clothing for decorating (A vest or hat might be a good smaller piece with which to start.)

many, many white buttons (These can be donated by people who have saved them over the years or inexpensive bagfuls can be purchased from hobby and sewing stores. Colorful buttons—ANY buttons—are fun to add to the project!)

needle and thread

fabric glue, optional

sewing scissors

Process

1. Spread the vest or lay the hat out on the work surface. Place some buttons on top of the clothing, arranging the buttons and rearranging until a pattern looks right. Begin simple. More can be added later.
2. Take the buttons off the clothing and set aside.
3. Thread the needle with the thread. A doubled piece of thread with a big knot at one end will work nicely. Start the thread on the back of the clothing so the knot doesn't show. Poke it through to the front, and slip a button hole over the needle and thread. Let it fall to the clothing. Now pierce the needle and thread back through the other button hole. Go in and out several times until the button is secure.
4. Without breaking the thread, poke the needle through the fabric from the back and add another button. Sew buttons until the thread is all gone. Then add more. Add more and more. (Buttons can also be glued on with fabric glue instead of sewing.)
5. Sew the buttons on the clothing in the original arrangement or create a design while sewing along. Wear the Pearlie outfit with pride!

▲ Note: This project could be stretched out over several weeks with a few buttons added each day until the clothing is filled with a Pearlie design.

ENGLAND

Did you know?

Around 1900 in London a group of people who sold fruit and other goods from wagons in the street started a custom to attract customers by sewing a line of buttons up the sides of their trousers. The vendors who decorated themselves with buttons were called Pearlies, because the buttons looked like pearls. Although there are few Pearlies left, they still attract a great deal of attention wherever they sell their wares.

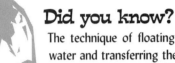

some experience   preparation   printing

Marbled Papers

ENGLAND

Did you know?

The technique of floating ink on water and transferring the design to paper was originally developed in Persia (the ancient country of Iran) in the 16th century. In the 18th century, an English Lord Chancellor of the Exchequer was responsible for the marbling paper technique being introduced in England. These papers were used by bookbinders who incorporated beautiful marbled papers as "end papers" in books, just inside the hard covers. Marbled end papers are still a traditional and popular design in bookbinding.

Young artists create a simplified version of marbled paper by floating an oil-based ink on water and then lifting the design onto paper.

Materials

latex gloves and big aprons to cover
shallow pan and water
oil-based ink (non-toxic varieties are available) with ink-dropper top (or use an eyedropper)
craft stick
any paper, cut to about 6" (15 cm) square, such as
    construction paper
    plain butcher paper
    thin matte boards
newspaper drying area

Process

1. Put on latex gloves and a good covering apron when working with oil-based ink. It is hard to wash off hands and clothing.
2. When ready, put the water in the shallow pan.
3. Drop several drops of colored ink on the water.
4. Very gently swirl the ink a little with a craft stick.
5. Fold the corner of a square of paper to make a little tab to use for a lifting corner.
6. Carefully float the paper square on top of the ink swirls and quickly but gently pull the paper off the surface of the inky water by the little folded corner. Do not let the paper soak.
7. Place the marbled paper on a drying area of thick newspaper. Dry overnight.
8. Make as many as desired. Add more ink drops as necessary.
9. When the squares are dry, use them to display and enjoy, as end sheets for little books or as note cards.

Quilling Paper Design

Young artists create a quilling design with a simple beginning idea such as geometric shapes.

Materials

construction paper or matte board for background
pencil
colored construction paper strips about ½" (1 cm) wide, variety of colors
glue

Process

1. Draw a simple shape such as a square, circle, triangle or diamond on a matte board or sheet of paper for the background.
2. Select a few of the ½" wide colored construction paper strips.
3. Hold one end of the strip around part of the rounded portion of a pencil. Roll the strip around the pencil so the strip is like a cinnamon roll. This may require some adult assistance until the artist gets the hang of it.
4. Slip the rolled paper strip off the pencil, keeping it rolled. (This reminds some of us of curling hair on rollers!)
5. Glue the rolled paper *on its side* to the construction design, either on the outline, inside the design or outside the design.
▲ Note: The paper should stay rolled, but may unroll a little, which is fine.
6. Continue rolling and gluing the paper curls until all of the design is quilled and filled in with rolls and curls. Dry completely.
7. Try a more complicated design project after exploring the simple one.
▲ Note: Strips of quilling paper can be purchased at craft stores.

ENGLAND

Did you know?

Quilling is the art of curling paper strips into rolled forms, and gluing them onto a background to make beautiful designs and textures. Although it is believed that the Egyptians were the first to begin quilling, the first clear reference to it as an art is found in England in the 15th century. At that time, it was used by poor church organizations to provide background for religious sculptures.

       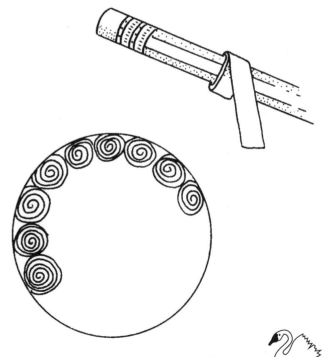

some experience   preparation   construction

Thaumatropes

ENGLAND

Did you know?

In 1825, Dr. Fitton invented a paper toy called a thaumatrope which used the idea of persistence of vision, or how one image on the retina of the eye is retained long enough for a second image to be superimposed on the first. The thaumatrope was a circular card with strings attached on opposite sides. One side was a picture of a bird, on the other side a picture of a bird's perch. When the card was whirled between the strings, it appeared that the bird was standing on the perch.

Young artists can make their own thaumatropes to enjoy and to amuse friends and family.

Materials

cardboard
colored markers
scissors
paper punch
string

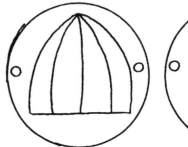 

Process

1. Draw a circle on the cardboard. Cut the circle out. (Cardboard can be difficult to cut, so adult assistance may be needed.)
2. Think of objects that go together like
   ✓ a fish and fish bowl
   ✓ a bird and a branch
   ✓ a person and a chair
   ✓ a smiling face and a picture frame
   ✓ a sleeping cat and a rug
3. Draw one object on each side of the circle.
4. Punch a hole in opposite sides of the circle, one on each side. Lace string through the holes.
5. Wind up the circle while holding the string stretched between both hands, and then let it go. It should whirl and show both pictures merging as one.

Simple Thaumatrope

Cut two circles out of heavy paper. Draw the thaumatrope ideas—such as the fish and fish bowl—one on each circle. Staple the circles, back to back, over a round stick or dowel. Rub the stick between the palms of the hands and the pictures can flip back and forth, causing the same thaumatrope effect as the spinning string.

Handmade Soap

Young artists make French hand soap from leftover recycled soap pieces.

Materials

double boiler and water
leftover soap pieces
stove
large spoon
perfume
cookie sheets
spatula
cookie cutters
paper towels

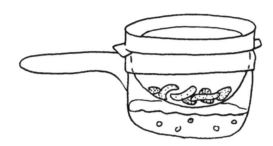

FRANCE

Did you know?

Soap is said to have been discovered in ancient Rome by mistake. But it was not until a French scientist discovered that soap could be made inexpensively that everyone began to buy it and use it. The French are famous for soap that is made into pretty, fancy shapes that are scented with lovely fragrances.

Process

▲ Note: All steps involving the stove must be assisted and supervised by an adult.

1. Fill the bottom of the double boiler about half full with water.
2. Put the soap pieces and a little water in the top part of the double boiler.
3. With adult help, place the double boiler on the stove on medium heat. As the soap warms and softens, stir it to smooth out any lumps. Add a little more water if necessary.
4. Stir in some perfume or heavily scented liquid bubble bath to add fragrance.
5. When the mixture becomes the consistency of thick oatmeal, with adult assistance pour it on a cookie sheet. Smooth it to about 1/8" (3 mm) thick with the spatula.
6. Allow it to cool and harden a few minutes.
7. Cut into the soap with the cookie cutters.
8. Remove the soap shapes with the spatula and place them on the paper towels.
9. Gather up the soap scraps, resoften them and follow the same process.

Gift Idea

The soap shapes can be wrapped in clear plastic and tied with a ribbon as a lovely and useful gift of handmade French soap.

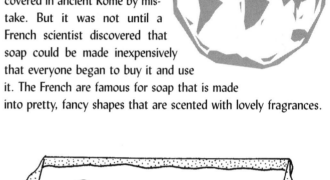

Profile Silhouette

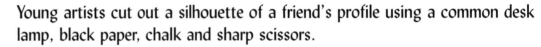

FRANCE

Did you know?

Although silhouette art was part of Roman culture, the French are credited with the side view or profile view of a person's head and shoulder. The silhouette is directly cut from a piece of paper and presented as a simple form of a portrait.

Young artists cut out a silhouette of a friend's profile using a common desk lamp, black paper, chalk and sharp scissors.

Materials

chair
adjustable desk lamp
table
tape
black paper
white chalk
good, sharp scissors
other paper and white glue

Process

1. Arrange a chair about a foot from the wall.
2. Then place the lamp a foot from the chair and arrange the lamp shining towards the wall. Test the lamp to see if it shines on the wall.
3. Tape the black paper to the wall where the light is shining.
4. Ask a friend to sit on the chair with one ear towards the wall and the other towards the light. Test the silhouette to find if the light shines to make a sharp outline of the person's profile. If it does not make a clear profile, rearrange the chair and the light.
5. The person must remain very still while the profile is traced. Trace the profile with white chalk.
6. After the profile is completed, cut out the profile on the chalk line.
7. Glue the profile to another sheet of paper of contrasting color such as white for the finished profile silhouette.

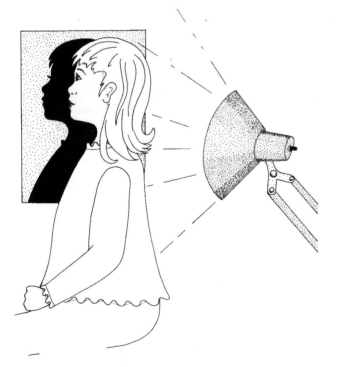

Beeswax Modeling

Young artists should not miss the opportunity to work with fragrant, soothing beeswax, perhaps to create little bumblebee sculptures or even a scene from a German fairy tale!

Materials

modeling beeswax in a variety of colors, available in school supply stores and fine art stores

Process

Basic modeling

1. Break a small piece of beeswax from the stick, perhaps about ¼ stick. Soften the small piece by warming it in the hands until it is pliable and warm. This is a good time to listen to a story, because it can take quite awhile. Mmmm, smell the honey hive?

▲ Caution: beeswax will melt if left in direct sunlight, in a car or near a heat source.

2. When the wax is softened, begin to shape the wax by pulling, rolling and flattening.
3. Make a shape or figure of any kind. Start with a snake or a cinnamon roll to explore how the beeswax feels.
4. Let the beeswax sculpture cool. It will harden and keep its shape until it is warmed and reshaped again. The beeswax can be used again and again.

Some ideas

Create a flower, bee or butterfly by pulling thin petals from a ball of wax.

Roll a coil to form a snake with eyes of a different color wax.

Mix beeswax to form marbled colors.

From an oval ball, pull legs, arms and head to make an animal like a dog or cat.

Knead the beeswax until it is a thin sheet and use it to cover other things like a small block of wood or a cardboard jewelry box.

Work as a group and create an entire scene with characters, garden, animals, etc.

GERMANY

Did you know?

A common art supply found in German schools for children is colored beeswax for modeling. This is a wonderful art medium that smells like honey as hands warm and shape it. Modeling beeswax comes in beautiful colors in stick shapes. It can take some time to soften the wax, but what a great time to listen to a German fairy tale!

some experience   preparation   construction

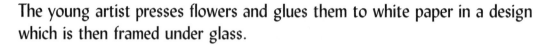

GERMANY

Did you know?

Germany has a long history of creating beautiful artwork with flowers. One of Germany's most beautiful flower crafts is pressing flowers for use on lovely custom designed stationary or framed designs.

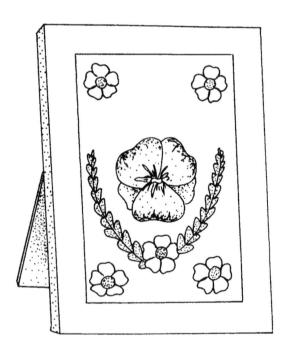

The young artist presses flowers and glues them to white paper in a design which is then framed under glass.

Materials

any flower blossoms and delicate leaves, such as any that are
    planted at home and grown from seeds
    collected outdoors from weeds or other flowers
    purchased from a flower shop
paper towels
sheet of cardboard, about 12″ x 18″ (30 cm x 45 cm)
heavy books
heavy paper or matte board (cut to fit in the picture frame)
white glue in a dish and toothpicks
empty picture frame with glass

Process

1. Gather flower blossoms and leaves in the early morning if possible.
2. Place the plant blossoms and delicate leaves between two paper towels on a sheet of cardboard. Leave space so plants are not touching each other.
3. Move the towels with the cardboard to an area where they will be undisturbed for several days. Place heavy books on top of the paper towels and flowers and leave several days.
4. Remove the books. Carry the flowers (still inside the towels) back to a work table. Lift the top paper towel to reveal the pressed flowers and leaves, but leave them undisturbed.
5. Gently select and lift a flower or leaf from the towel and place it on a sheet of paper. Arrange this flower or leaf, and then add others to the design. Be careful of gusts of wind or breezes made from people walking by which could accidentally blow the design off the paper.
6. When an arrangement is ready, dip the tip of a toothpick into the white glue and use a small dot of glue to stick a flower or leaf to the paper. Progress through all the flowers and leaves, gluing them with small dots to the paper. Soon all the leaves and flowers will be glued in place. Let the flower arrangement and glue dry completely.
7. Place the flower arrangement in the picture frame and enjoy the display though the clear glass for years and years.

Imaginary Mapmaking

drawing

1
preparation

experienced

Young artists design a map of a world based on pure imagination.

Materials

large sheet of drawing paper
something round to trace to fit the paper, such as a mixing bowl or a hula hoop
choice of coloring tools, such as
    paints and paintbrushes
    markers
    crayons
    pencils

Process

1. Place the large paper on the floor or on a table.
2. Place the circle shape, such as a bowl, in the center of the paper. (If the paper is VERY large, trace a hula hoop.) Trace around the circle shape with a marker or other drawing tool. Remove the shape. A circle for the shape of the planet will remain.
3. Next, imagine an entire world or planet that has not yet been discovered. Imagine the land shapes, the water shapes, where the mountains would be, where people would live. Would this be a planet for people or other creatures? Would this planet have land or be completely under water? Is this planet different from planet Earth?
4. Draw the imaginary world on the circle of paper. Put in as many details as desired. Paths, roads, houses, boats, creatures and other imaginary ideas might be fun to add to the drawing.
5. For extra fun, name the planet. Make up a story about it, too.

GERMANY

Did you know?

Two German mapmakers are known for setting a standard of excellence for mapmaking long ago. The oldest map of a globe was made by German merchant and navigator Martin Behaim (1459-1507). Another large map of the world was drawn by Martin Waldseemüller (1470-1518), printed on 12 sheets and measuring 4½' x 8' (1.5 x 2.5 m). Each separate sheet was printed from a woodcut.

beginner   preparation   sculpture

Bread Dough Coins

GREECE

Did you know?

From the earliest times, people have used salt, nails, stones, whale teeth, shells and almost anything imaginable as money. Gradually people began to use gold, silver and jewelry as money in manageable and convenient shapes and sizes. The Chinese were among the first to use coins, but the Greeks were the first to add art to their coins. They stamped pictures of rulers, leaders, heroes, architecture, religion, art and athletic events on every coin.

Young artists work up a dough from stale bread to make cookie-shaped coins they can paint.

Materials

white bread, stale (two slices per artist)
bowl
white glue
aluminum foil
small, round cookie cutter
food coloring and paintbrushes

Process

1. Tear the crusts off the bread. Discard or use to feed the birds.
2. Tear the bread into small pieces and place them in the bowl. Add enough white glue to make the bread somewhat wet, but not overly runny.
3. With fingers, mash the bread and glue together to make a dough-like mixture. If needed, add more glue. (Too much glue? Add more bread.)
4. Hand roll the dough into balls. Then flatten each ball on aluminum foil with fingers.
5. Use the cookie cutter to cut the dough balls into small circles.
6. Leave the circles on the foil. Paint designs or pictures on the bread dough coins with food coloring.
7. Let them dry until hard.

Button Coins

With the help of an adult, young artists make a replica of an ancient coin with polymer clay and buttons.

Materials

small lump of any polymer clay, such as Sculpey or Fimo
several buttons (try to find decorative metal buttons with a design in the round top)
metallic colored polymer clay (in silver, gold and copper colors)
pencil or straightened paper clip
baking sheet and oven mitts
oven preheated to 250°F (130°C)

Process

1. Flatten some clay to a 1" (3 cm) thick slab. Press buttons into the clay to make impressions. Let this clay mold harden completely by leaving it out in the air for 1 or 2 days.
2. Next, soften a small lump of metallic clay by squeezing it by hand, and gently press a bit of the metallic clay into each button impression.
3. Insert the point of a pencil or straightened paper clip into the back of the metallic colored clay and lift each clay coin out of the mold. Place on the baking sheet.
4. With adult help, bake the metallic-colored clay coins in an oven following the directions on the clay package (usually for 5–10 minutes at 250°F).
5. Cool on the baking sheet. The baked cooled coins will be hard and shiny like real metal coins.

Variation

To make a crayon-wax coin

1. Peel the paper off a metallic crayon and break it into small pieces. An adult melts the crayon pieces in a small metal cup set in a pan of very hot water.
▲ Caution: Adult help and supervision is needed. Wax is flammable if it gets too hot. Never melt wax directly over a burner or flame; use a pan of hot water.
2. When the wax is melted, an adult pours the liquid wax into the impressions made in the clay.
3. When the wax cools completely, pop the wax coins out of the clay mold.

GREECE

Did you know?

The ancient Greeks, around 100 BC, made coins out of precious metals like silver and gold. Each Greek city made its own coins, as it was a sign of great power for a city to mint its own money.
Images of Greek gods, animals and famous people were used to decorate the coins. Coin artists carved small scenes into blocks of stone, then poured molten metal into the carved areas. When the metal cooled and hardened, the coin could be tipped out of the mold.

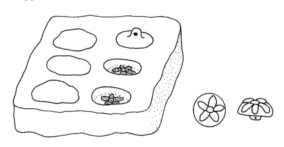

Walled City

GREECE

Did you know?

Hippodamos was a local architect who lived in the Greek city of Miletus around 470 BC. He designed and planned towns on a grand scale, with open spaces, public buildings and straight streets intersecting at right angles. A beautiful example of his town planning was Priene, across from Miletus, high on a sloping hilltop above the bay. Surrounded with a fortification wall to protect it from invasion, the town was beautifully planned for living, working and playing.

Industrious, motivated young artists plan and build a town of milk cartons in the style of Hippodamos, the famous Greek architect.

Materials

large sheet of cardboard to cover a table
boxes to act as buildings, such as

milk cartons (small and large)	jewelry boxes
dry food boxes	shoe boxes

glue, masking tape, stapler, other materials for attaching and building
tempera paint and brushes, markers and crayons
scraps, such as

construction paper	butcher or craft paper
magazine pages	cardboard scraps
foil or clear plastic wrap	wrapping paper

Process

1. Unfold or cut a piece of cardboard for the base of the town.
2. Talk about and plan the possibilities for the town. The town can be small or large, ancient or modern, real or imaginary. Think: Will there be a park, a pond, a theater, a stadium, shops and stores, schools, playgrounds? Where will the houses or apartments be? When the plans are begun, draw them out on the cardboard. Draw streets too.
3. When all the streets are drawn, begin building the town's houses and buildings. Milk cartons and boxes work well and can be covered with colored paper. Windows, doors, bricks and other decorations can be drawn on the paper that covers them. Sloped roofs can be made by folding a rectangle of paper and taping it over the top of the milk carton or box. Small signs can be made for stores. Columns can be made from rolled paper for a colonnade.
4. Add other town necessities to the design. Aluminum foil or plastic wrap can be used to symbolize water such as ponds or rivers. Construct trees and flowers, if desired. Paint the streets and lawns.
5. When the town structure seems almost complete, use long pieces of cardboard scraps and masking tape to build a fortification wall around the entire town.
6. For extra fun, add action figures or toy characters such as people and animals to the town.

Double Roller Painting

Young artists explore the concept of the ball-point pen by filling deodorant bottles with thin tempera paint and painting on paper.

Materials

2 empty roll-on deodorant bottles
soap and water
paper towels
thin tempera paints in two colors
masking tape
paper

Process

1. With adult help, remove the roller part of the deodorant bottles.
2. Clean the bottles thoroughly with soap and water. Dry with a paper towel.
3. Put some tempera paint in each bottle.
4. With adult help, replace the roller on the deodorant bottle.
5. Do the same for another color of tempera paint.
6. Stand the deodorant bottles upright on a table.
7. Tape the bottles together side by side (see the illustration).
8. Turn the joined bottles upside down and roll them on the paper to draw, write or make designs—just like the invention of the ball-point pen, but double the fun!

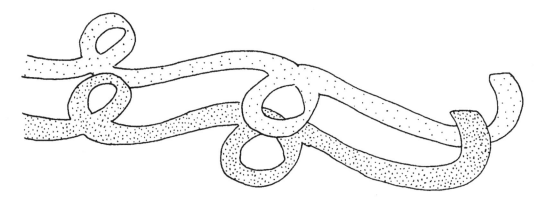

HUNGARY

Did you know?

The first ball-point pen was invented in Hungary in 1935 by brothers Lazlo and Georg Biro. It was a tube filled with ink, with a tiny metal ball in the tip. Ink from a cartridge inside the pen sticks to the ball as it rolls across the paper, spreading ink in a line. The first model had a roller like a rolling pin in the tip, but there was a problem—that pen could only write in straight lines!

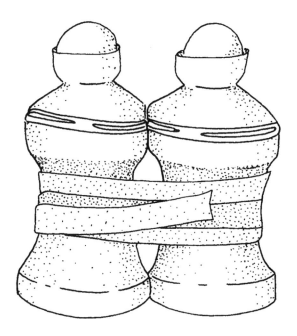

beginner

1

preparation

painting

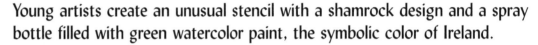

Sprayed Shamrock Stencils

IRELAND

Did you know?

The shamrock is a green plant with a clover-like leaf shape that has become symbolic of Ireland, like the maple leaf is to Canada or the hibiscus to Hawaii. The shamrock is an important symbol on St. Patrick's Day, a traditional Irish holiday.

Young artists create an unusual stencil with a shamrock design and a spray bottle filled with green watercolor paint, the symbolic color of Ireland.

Materials

pencil and heavy paper
scissors
masking tape
large sheet of butcher paper
green liquid watercolor paint (or thin green tempera paint) in spray bottles (other selections of colors may be used too)
spatula, optional

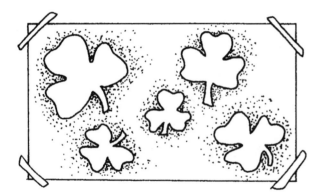

Process

1. Draw a shamrock on the heavy paper. Draw it fairly large, about 6" (15 cm) across. As an optional idea, make numerous shamrocks in a variety of sizes.
2. Cut the shamrock out (or cut all the shamrocks out).
3. Make a loop of masking tape and stick the shamrock (or shamrocks) to the large sheet of butcher paper.
4. Tape the butcher paper to a wall or paint easel.
5. Spray the shamrock and surrounding paper with a fine spray of green paint. Dry briefly.
6. For an optional effect, take a spatula and scrape the sprayed paint with the edge of the spatula, smearing it in designs. Scrape over the stencil, but be careful not to catch the edge of the shamrock or it might tear. Work gently.
7. Peel off the shamrock (or shamrocks) and see the stencil designs left behind.

Additional paint idea

Stick the shamrocks on the dry green paint. Spray them with another, new color and repeat the same effect. This will produce a dual-colored stencil design.

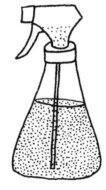

Fancy Eyeglasses

Young artists can get a little silly and creative when they decorate old eyeglass frames with fancy feathers, buttons and hobby jewels for a high fashion eye-wear show.

Materials

old eyeglass frames
soap, hot water and towel
tacky glue
decorative materials such as
    feathers
    buttons
    sequins
    glitter
    ribbon
    hobby jewels
    beads
    colored paper
cool gluegun, optional

Process

1. Find an old pair of eyeglass frames without lenses, or ask an adult to remove the lenses. Wash the frames in hot soapy water to remove oils and grime. Dry with a clean towel.
2. Create a fancy pair of glasses using decorative materials like feathers, buttons, glitter and other collected items. Glue the items on the glasses with a good tacky glue. (A cool-touch glue gun would work well here, with adult assistance.)
3. Let the glasses and glue dry completely.
4. Wear the glasses! Have an eyeglass fashion show or parade!

ITALY

Did you know?

The Roman emperor Nero was the first to use a type of eyeglass to aid his vision. He discovered that a precious stone mounted on a ring could act like a magnifying glass! Although many people first objected to them, they soon found eyeglasses to be useful because they could see so much better! Eyeglasses also became a source of high fashion throughout the social circles of Europe. Monocles—glasses with only one lens for one eye—were especially popular.

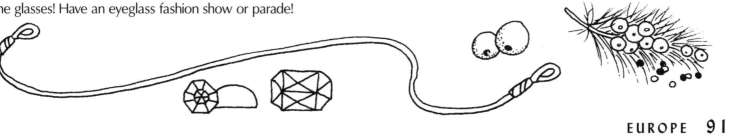

some experience | preparation | collage | caution

Ironed Crayon Mosaics

ITALY

Did you know?

Mosaics are an ancient form of art made by fitting small pieces of glass, tiles, stones or precious jewels together in a picture or design. In Italy, these colored designs are called *tesserae* and usually consist of marble pieces for floors and glass pieces for walls. The most famous mosaic was unearthed by archeologists in the ruins of Pompeii, a city of the ancient Roman Empire covered in lava by a volcanic eruption.

Young artists create the stones for their mosaics from scraps of melted crayon broken into bits, then glued on a background.

Materials

old iron
sheets of newspaper
wax paper
old crayon stubs, peeled
matte board and glue
tempera paint and paintbrush

Process

1. Plug in the iron to preheat to medium. Place some newspaper on a work surface next to the iron.
▲ Note: Adult assistance is needed for all ironing steps.
2. Spread several thicknesses of wax paper on the newspaper. Drop chunks and bits of a variety of colors of old crayons on the wax paper. Cover the wax paper with several more sheets of wax paper. Cover all with a sheet of newspaper.
3. Iron the crayon scraps, melting them slowly. They will take on a marbled look by the mixing of the colors. Cool until hard. (Put them in the refrigerator for a speedy cooling process.)
4. Open the sheets of wax paper and peel away the crayon blobs. Break the blobs into smaller pieces.
5. Glue these crayon pieces onto the matte board in a pattern or random design. Leave a little space between the pieces, if desired. Dry thoroughly.
6. Paint in the spaces between the crayon bits with tempera paint.

Variations

✓ Sketch a simple design on the matte board and glue on the bits to form a design.
✓ Melt single, unmixed colors of crayon in blobs. Break up and use as above.

Quill Pen

The young artist must find a good feather and then cut the tip of the quill end in a special way to make a working pen. All that's needed to complete the job is a little ink and a fresh piece of paper.

Materials

strong feather
scissors
ink in a bottle
paper

Process

1. Snip the tip of the quill off at a slight angle with the scissors. (See illustration for steps 1–3.)
2. Split the quill through the middle of the shaft about ½" (13 mm) up. Then cut away the side part.
3. Sharpen the remaining part of the quill into a point with the scissors.
4. Dip the point into the ink. Tap off any excess ink on the side of the bottle.
5. Draw lightly to make marks by lightly pressing the quill point on the paper while moving the pen.
6. Dip the pen in ink again whenever more ink is need. When the point dulls, wash off the ink and cut the tip again to sharpen it.
7. Draw or write with the quill pen, just like people did long ago.
▲ Note: If ink is not readily available, or for variety, substitute other colored liquids, such as
   ✓ fresh squeezed juice of raspberries
   ✓ strong food coloring in a shallow dish
   ✓ dark purple grape juice
   ✓ watercolor paint mixed strong in a shallow dish
   ✓ fabric dye mixed strong in a shallow dish

INK

ITALY

Did you know?

During the Middle Ages in Italy, important business was recorded with a reed quill on a papyrus leaf. This combination of materials lead to the development of the quill pen, used for centuries as the most common type of writing instrument. The quill pen was primarily made of a large, strong feather taken from a goose, crow or raven.

1.

2.

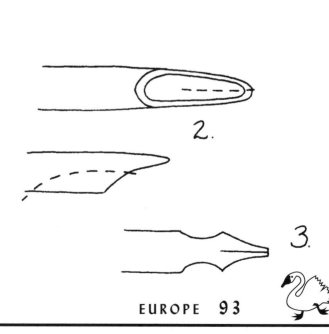

3.

Lapland Felt Square

LAPPS,
NORWAY, SWEDEN,
FINLAND & RUSSIA

Did you know?

The Lapps are a tribe from the northernmost areas of four countries: Norway, Sweden, Finland and Russia. Some are still nomadic and spend a good portion of the year following the migration of reindeer herds through the coldest parts of Europe and Russia near the Arctic Circle, an area called Lapland. Lapps wear bright blue clothing bordered with brilliant red and yellow felt bands that are easy to see as they travel across the dazzling white snow.

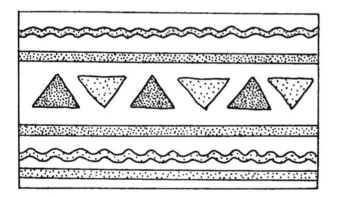

Young artists create a felt square design of red and yellow on a blue background, imitating the patterns of clothing worn by Lapps.

Materials
scraps of bright red and yellow felt
pencil
ruler
scissors
square of bright blue felt
sewing scraps and trims, optional, such as
    rickrack
    braid
    seam binding
white glue or fabric glue
sewing pins, optional

Process
1. Draw and cut out triangles of red and yellow felt. Use a pencil and ruler if desired to draw the shapes. If there are enough scraps, cut a band of yellow and of red.
2. Arrange the triangles and bands on the bright blue felt square in a pattern. Move pieces about until satisfied with the pattern. Add rickrack and braid if desired. .
3. When the pattern is complete, glue the felt pieces and any trim to the blue felt square. Use pins to hold, if needed.
4. Dry overnight.
5. Use the felt square to display on a wall, as a table cover or to enjoy in any way desired.

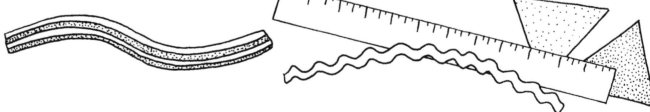

Ice Skating Painting

Young artists can imagine ice skating on the frozen canals of the Netherlands as they etch ice skating designs in crayon and then paint over the design with ice blue paint.

Materials

heavy white paper
dark blue crayons, various shades
scratching tool, such as
   a fingernail, paper clip, spoon tip or ballpoint pen with the point pulled in
frosty blue tempera paint in a cup (thinned with a little water)
wide, soft paintbrush

Process

1. Draw a circle or pond shape on the heavy white paper.
2. Color the pond with different shades of dark blue crayon until the pond is filled.
3. With a fingernail or other scratching tool, scrape ice skating designs in the pond. Some typical skating designs are shown in the illustrations, such as figure-eights, scallops, loops and curls. Don't forget some dots for toe picks!
4. To complete the icy design, mix some water with frosty blue tempera paint in a cup for a paint wash.
5. With a wide soft paintbrush, paint frosty blue paint over the entire design. Then dry. The painting will look like a frozen pond that not long before occupied fancy ice skaters.

Another icy idea

Cut the pond out and paste it on a sheet of white paper to resemble snow surrounding an icy pond. Cut out evergreen trees and paste around the pond like a skating scene. The trees can be made to "stand." Glue a toy skater figure onto the design, such as those used for decorating cakes.

NETHERLANDS (HOLLAND)

Did you know?

Although evidence of ice skating in 50 BC was found among the Roman ruins in London, it was not until 1250 AD that iron blades were first developed and used in the Netherlands. The Dutch became the greatest developer of ice skates and skating styles. In the 1300's, skates were developed that had highly waxed wooden blades. Steel blades appeared in 1400 making skates lighter and skating easier.

Shell Decorating

NETHERLANDS (HOLLAND)

Did you know?

Because of their proximity to the sea, the Dutch observed and greeted merchants and vessels from all over the world. In the Netherlands, architects were able to place orders for large quantities of common varieties of shells needed for decorating; architects often emphasized the details of their work with inlayed shell designs. For example, the decorating of grottoes with shells became the fad of the middle 18th century.

Young artists decorate a small gift box with a selection of special collected shells.

Materials

seashells (collected or purchased)
soap and water
paper towels
small box to decorate, such as
   jewelry box
   cigar box
   gift box
   wooden box
white or hobby glue
paintbrush

Process

1. Clean the shells in soap and water and let them dry on the paper towels.
2. Sort the shells according to their physical attributes like color, size and shape.
3. Squeeze a dot or small puddle of glue on a section of the box.
4. Place a shell on the glue dot and hold briefly until it holds.
5. Then find another shell and place it in some glue on the box.
6. Continue gluing the shells until the entire box is covered. Paint over the shells with a little more glue to make them shiny.
7. Dry overnight, and use the box as a way to display the shells.

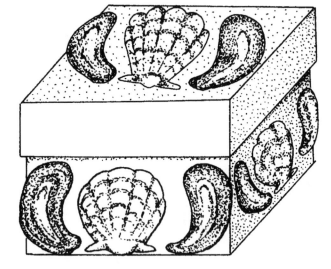

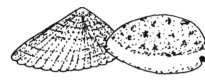

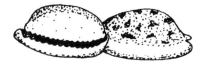

Rosemaling on a Cardboard Chest

Young artists explore rosemaling and paint a rose design on a white cardboard box that can be made into a storage chest.

Materials

paper, pencil, crayons
cardboard box with lid (the kind that reams of copy paper come in)
non-toxic acrylic paint and paintbrushes
jar of water for rinsing brushes and a rag
cloth tape

Process

1. Look at an illustration of a rose. Practice a rose design like the illustration—or a completely new design—on the piece of paper. Color it in with crayons, if desired.
2. Paint this rose design (or another design) on the cardboard box lid. Paint as many roses as desired. Keep the paintbrush rinsed for bright clear colors. Dry.
3. Tape the box lid to the box on one side like hinges so the lid will lift and fall. Paint a lock on the latching side for fun.
4. Use the box as a chest.
5. Ideas of other things to paint with rosemaling designs

| gift box | wooden board | chair | wooden box |
| paper | matte board | table | cardboard box |

NORWAY

Did you know?

One of the best known crafts of Norway is rosemaling, the art of "rose painting." In the 1700's, rosemalers (men who painted rose designs) traveled from home to home painting walls, ceilings, furniture and chests with their individual techniques and designs. Although the styles of rosemaling were often regionally unique, the colors were always similar in bright blue, bright red, gold and dark green, with accents of black or white.

POLAND

Did you know?

The Polish people developed a charming new folk craft from the tradition of making cutouts from leather and cloth, called the Polish Wycinanka Ludowa—the paper cut. Polish peasants used this folk craft to decorate their homes by cutting glossy paper using sheep shears. The folk craft progressed into an art form. Designs can be very simple or extremely intricate. These paper cuts must be symmetrical, meaning that when folded in half, the design is exactly the same on one side as on the other side.

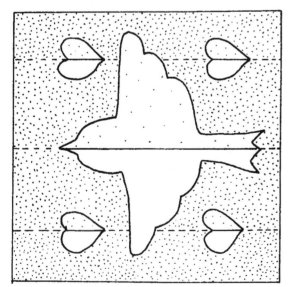

Young artists experiment with simple cutout transparencies and progress to a more complex cutout paper scene.

SIMPLE TRANSPARENCY

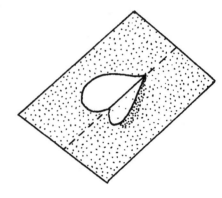

Materials

sheets of glossy paper or oragami paper
pencil
scissors
art tissue
glue

Process

1. Fold the glossy sheet of paper in half.
2. Draw a shape on the folded edge of the glossy paper. Drawing half of a symmetrical shape will give a full shape when the paper is opened.
3. Cut along the lines of the drawn shape. Do not cut the fold. (Shapes can be cut free-hand without drawing lines first, if desired.) Unfold the cut shape. Fold it back so it stands up from the paper.
4. Fold the paper again across a different part of the paper that has not been used yet. Cut another shape from the fold, and then fold it back so it stands.
5. Continue folding and cutting shapes from wherever there is room on the paper.
6. For a final touch, glue pieces of colored art tissue on the back of the paper cutout to cover the cutout shapes. The light will shine through the tissue and make the colors seem even brighter.
7. Hang the Simple Transparency in a window or wherever a light source shines brightly to show off the paper cutouts backed by bright tissue.

Transparency Scene

Materials

sheets of glossy paper or origami paper
pencil
scissors
glue
art tissue or colored paper

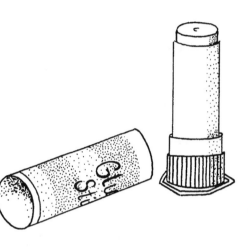

Process

1. Think of a scene or picture, such as
   ✓ fish under the sea
   ✓ flower garden filled with blossoms
   ✓ house with tree, sky and sun
   ✓ rocket to outer space
   The undersea scene will be used for this project description, but feel free to choose any idea.
2. Fold the paper and lightly sketch a half of a fish on the paper. Cut on the lines and fold the cutout up from the paper. It should look like a whole fish when folded back. Glue the folded fish down so the cutout hole is completely open.
3. Draw and cut as many fish for the scene in this manner as desired, gluing each one down to stay open.
4. Now add some seaweed or plants. Draw half of a wiggly strand of seaweed. Cut it out and fold it back for a complete and wide piece of seaweed. Glue down.
5. Add anything else to the undersea scene that is symmetrical, such as bubbles or starfish, cutting half of the shape, fold it back the other half of the shape, and glue down.
6. Glue the paper cutout scene to another piece of colored paper or a piece of art tissue so the colors show through the open cutouts.
7. Display on a wall or in a window.

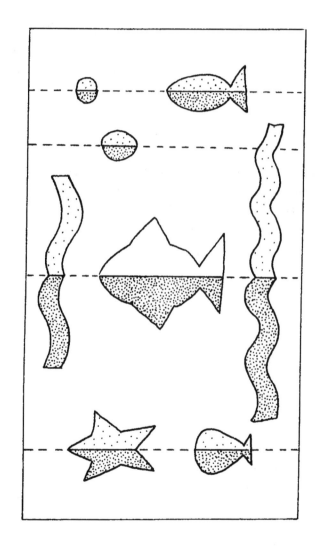

Matryoshka Doll Boxes

RUSSIA

Did you know?

A traditional Russian toy is the nesting doll set, or matryoshka dolls. They are hollow wooden dolls shaped a little like bowling pins, each a little larger than the next. Matryoshka means grandmother, and the dolls look like traditional Russian grandmothers with the babushka head scarves they wear. Sets may have four or five dolls or as many as twenty or more nesting in one set. Dolls may be simply painted in traditional bright red and blue or may be more elaborate, even gilded with real gold.

Young artists make a nesting set of gift boxes decorated to look like little people.

Materials

4 to 8 different-sized gift boxes with lids (ones that nest inside one another)
▲ Note: Unpainted wooden nesting matryoshka dolls are available at some hobby and craft stores at a reasonable price.
colored markers
scraps of paper
scissors
glue

Process

1. Draw and color the smallest box to look like a matryoshka doll.
2. Next, copy the matryoshka doll design on the next to the smallest box.
3. Decorate all of the boxes with matryoshka dolls until all of the boxes are colored.
4. Go back and glue scraps of paper to the boxes to decorate the dolls. For example, cut and glue a red scrap for an apron on each doll or a little flower scrap for a scarf. Let the glue dry.
5. Nest the boxes, one inside the another. Open and display all in a row, or keep nested in the largest box.

Theme Design Ideas
Design boxes with any characters that fit a theme, such as the following
✓ Fairy Tales: with four boxes, make one for each of the characters in a fairy tale, such as the wolf, the woodcutter, the grandma and Little Red Riding Hood.
✓ Family: assign a box to each family member, from Dad down to the goldfish.
✓ Circus: decorate boxes to match circus animals or characters, from biggest to smallest.
✓ Garden: decorate each box like a flower in a garden.
✓ Animals: decorate each box to show the food chain, with the biggest, hungriest animal on the largest box, and the littlest animal on the smallest box.

Jeweled Eggs

Young artists decorate a lovely jeweled egg, perhaps beginning a new tradition at home or school.

Materials

raw egg
darning needle
bowl
paper towels
scissors
glue
decorations, such as

sequins	metallic glitter glue	hobby faux jewels
old beads	glitter	metallic thread
metallic glitter	gold and silver rickrack	colored sand

small piece of play clay

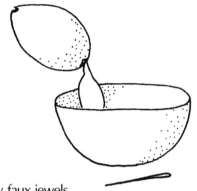

Process

1. Hold the larger end of the egg carefully in one hand. Pierce a hole in the top of the egg with the darning needle.
2. Turn the egg upside down and pierce a hole in the opposite end. Move the needle around inside this hole to make it a little larger than the other.
3. Hold the egg over a bowl and blow into the small hole to make the insides come out through the larger hole. If the insides won't come out, shake the egg to break the yoke or poke the needle in the yoke. Blow again. Save the insides to make scrambled eggs, an omelet or a cake.
4. Rinse the egg well under running water, letting water rinse through the inside of the egg too. Dry on paper towels.
5. When the egg is dry, glue the jewels and other glittery decorations on the egg in a beautiful design.
6. Display on a small piece of play clay as a stand.

RUSSIA

Did you know?

Emperor Alexander III of Russia asked the young jeweler Peter Carl Fabergé to make the first Imperial Easter egg. When the egg was complete, the emperor was very surprised at its beauty; it was decorated with priceless jewels and gold. He was so pleased that he asked Fabergé to continue to make a special egg each Easter, beginning the tradition of the Fabergé Eggs, which are collected by people all over the world.

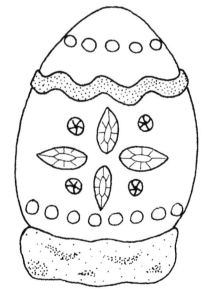

beginner preparation construction

Simple Kaleidoscope

SCOTLAND

Did you know?

Sir David Brewster, a famous Scottish scientist, invented the kaleidoscope in 1813. Sir Brewster was fascinated with science in his childhood, especially with light. When he grew up, he became a scientist and experimented with colors and light. During these experiments, he developed the kaleidoscope, a viewing tube with mirrors which create an ever-changing six-sided design.

Young artists construct the simple workings of the inside of a kaleidoscope with shiny, silvery Mylar plastic.

Materials

shiny Mylar plastic
scissors
cloth tape, or any tape

Process

1. Cut the Mylar into three strips about 2″ wide by 6″ long (5 cm x 15 cm). Adult help may be needed.
2. Tape the strips together along the long edges of the plastic to form a triangular tube shape.
3. Hold the tube up to one eye like a telescope and look at an object. How many objects can be seen? Look all around. Try turning and twisting the tube and see what happens.

Other Viewing Ideas

✓ Glue a colorful cellophane square between cardboard frames and look through it.
✓ Glue a square of art tissue on a cardboard frame. Then glue another square of tissue that has been cut into a fancy shape or snowflake on top of the first. Add a second frame to sandwich them in. Look through it when dry.
✓ Glue strips or shapes of aluminum foil on a black posterboard square. Reflect sunlight or a flashlight beam off the design card and onto a wall (or into a mirror).
✓ Walk backwards looking over the shoulder through a make-up mirror.
✓ Choose a piece of art—with words, painted, drawn or collage—and look at it through the kaleidoscope tube, hold it up to a mirror or look at it through the cellophane viewer.

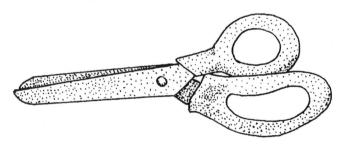

Portable Gardens

construction   preparation   some experience

Young artists design and plant a portable garden or terrarium in a large plastic bottle using plants they have grown or collected from outdoors.

Materials

large clear plastic or glass bottle, with a wide mouth and lid
small pebbles and charcoal bits from pet stores
garden peat, potting soil and bowl
a choice of three small plants, such as any of the following
    dug up from outdoors with dirt clinging to roots
    grown from seeds in milk cartons beforehand
    purchased from a garden store
spoon and fork
spray bottle filled with water
indirect light source, on a shelf or window sill (not direct sun)

Process

1. Put a layer of pebbles in the bottom of the container.
2. Then layer the charcoal bits on top of the pebbles.
3. Mix the peat and the soil together in a bowl. Add the mixture to the charcoal and press it down in an even layer.
4. Next, dig three small holes suitable for the root ball of each plant.
5. Use the spoon and fork to gently lower the plants with their roots and dirt into the holes in the soil mixture.
6. Scoop the soil mixture back around the root areas. Press and pat them into place. Spray the plants with the water.
7. Screw the lid on the portable garden and put it in an area which gets light but not direct sun. Closing the lid on the terrarium helps the moisture condense and keep the plants naturally moist, like a small greenhouse.
8. Water once a week, to start, to keep the plants thriving. Then, water as necessary. Move the portable garden to different areas in the house and see how the plants respond to new and different light and locations.

SCOTLAND

Did you know?

In 1825 Alan Maconochie, a famous Scottish botanist, designed a tiny indoor greenhouse which sat in the window of his home and provided abundant flourishing plants for all to view. These small gardens could be moved easily and enjoyed in different locations. The idea caught on and now we call the little gardens terrariums.

peat and soil mixture

charcoal

pebbles

Print & Sculpt With Corks

SPAIN

Did you know?

Cork is a lightweight spongy material that comes from the bark of the cork oak tree, found in Spain, the world's most abundant source of cork. The cork oak must be at least 20 years old before its bark is removed to harvest cork. One of the products of cork is cork shavings which are burned to make Spanish black or cork black that is a paint for artists.

Young artists have many choices of art ideas using cork, including cork prints and cork sculptures, both easy enough for the youngest artists.

Materials

For Cork Prints

corks from bottles, in different sizes
tempera paint in a shallow dish
paper

For Cork Sculpture

corks from bottles, in different sizes
matte board
white glue (or cool-touch glue gun)
collage items to add to the sculpture

Process

Cork Prints

1. Dip either of the cork ends in the tempera paint.
2. Press the cork on paper several times to make prints.
3. When the paint imprints are faint, dip the cork back in the paint and continue making imprints until satisfied with the design. Then dry.
4. Make as many cork prints as desired. Consider using more than one color paint and many different sizes of corks.
▲ Note: Corks can also be cut into shapes with adult assistance, much like cutting a potato for a potato print.

Cork Sculpture

1. Collect and save all kinds of corks.
2. Place a matte board square on the table.
3. Glue a cork to the matte board. Then glue as many corks to the matte board and to each other as desired. Add collage items to the sculpture for interest and design.
4. When satisfied with the design, let the sculpture dry.
▲ Note: White glue dries slowly, so feel free to use tape to hold the corks together until the glue sets. Using a glue gun avoids the drying problem, but requires one-on-one adult assistance.

Salsa Rosa Necklace (Spiced Rose)

caution | sculpture | preparation | some experience

Young artists make a string of scented beads from fresh rose petals and cinnamon—a fragrant Spanish necklace.

Materials

darning needle and heavy string
fresh rose petals
measuring cup, 4 cup (1 liter) size
sauce pan with lid
water to cover petals in pan
stove

mesh strainer
cinnamon
spoon
baking sheet
oven preheated to 275°F (140°C)

Process

1. With adult help, thread a long piece of heavy string on a darning needle. Tie a knot at the end of the string. The string should be long enough to make a necklace that slips over the artist's head. Set aside.
2. Pull the petals from live cut roses. Measure 4 cups (1 L) of petals.
3. Pour the petals into the saucepan. Cover the petals with a little water. With adult supervision, bring the rose petals to a boil. Cover. Simmer until mushy and soft (a few minutes).
4. Place the mesh strainer over the large measuring cup. Pour the petals and water into the strainer, letting the water drip through to the cup below. Discard the water.
5. Scoop the petals into the large measuring cup. Sprinkle ¼ cup (50 g) or so of cinnamon over the petals. Mix and mash the cinnamon and rose petals together with the spoon. When well mixed, use hands to further mix and mash the petals and cinnamon into a dough.
▲ Note: The dough should hold together. If too dry, add a few drops of water. If too wet, add more cinnamon or a little flour.
6. Pinch off some of the dough and form a ball. Poke the ball with the darning needle. Pull the bead all the way to the end of the knotted string. Then tie another knot before adding more beads. Make another bead and pull it to the second knot. Tie another knot. Add another bead. Tie a knot. Do this until the string is filled with beads with knots in between each one.
7. Stretch out the string on the baking sheet. With adult help, bake for about 15 minutes at 275°F (140°C) until the beads are hard. Remove from the oven and cool on the baking sheet.
8. Tie the two loose ends of the necklace together and slip over the head. Enjoy the spicy Spanish fragrance!

SPAIN

Did you know?

Spain is a colorful country, with vividly costumed bull-fights, bright sunny climate and resplendent traditional clothing. The typical historical costume of a Spanish woman might consist of an elaborate ruffled dress, a headcovering called a mantilla (man-teé-ya) and a colorful bead necklace.

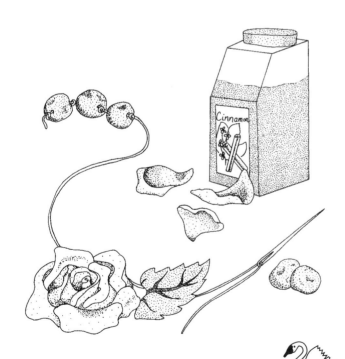

Hand Painted Tiles

SPAIN & PORTUGAL

Did you know?

It has been a tradition in Spain and Portugal to decorate homes with hand-painted glazed tiles in bright designs. Home decor includes tiled floors, walls, trims around doors and windows, table tops, courtyards, kitchens and baths. Tiles often show an Arabic or Moorish influence with geometric shapes such as triangles, squares and diamonds. Often nature is shown with vines and leaves.

The young artist hand paints a tile and bakes it in a kiln for permanent lasting beauty.

Materials

tile square, unglazed white, about 6″ x 6″ (15 cm x 15 cm), or any size desired
▲ Note: Bisque tiles are tiles that are ready to paint; they are usually available from hobby and craft stores.
paper plate
non-toxic clay paints or glazes
paintbrushes, one for each color
blow dryer
kiln
▲ Note: Ask a local high school or college art department to use their kiln.
pieces of cork, optional

Process

1. Purchase tiles in an unglazed bisque stage, ready to glaze with non-toxic clay paints.
2. Use a paper plate as a palette. Pour small puddles of non-toxic clay paint on the paper plate.
3. Paint and cover the entire tile with one color of paint. Use white or clear if a white tile is desired. Each layer or application of paint must be dry before adding more, so blow dry with a hair dryer between painting steps, or air dry.
4. Dip a paintbrush into a selected color and paint a design on the tile. Blow dry.
5. Add more designs and colors. Blow dry.
6. An adult bakes the completed tiles in a kiln to a permanent, glossy shine.

Where to use hand-painted tiles

Use as a trivet or a simple decoration. Glue little pieces of cork or felt on the back of the tile to prevent table or shelf from scratching. Many tiles can be set in cement or grout and used to cover a table, trim around a doorway or any number of other decorative ideas.

Straw Ornaments

Young artists bundle, weave, bend and construct straw into simple ornaments, or design their own unique ornaments, all with red string—just like the children in Sweden.

Materials

covered work area
yellow straw
pan of water
scissors
red string

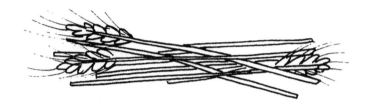

SWEDEN

Did you know?

Christmas is celebrated on Christmas Eve in Sweden. Straw ornaments are a significant part of Swedish Christmas decorations. The star decoration is a popular shape. Straw is collected and then tied in designs with red string.

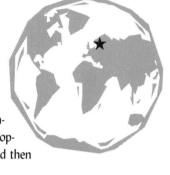

Process

Straw Bundles Ornament

1. Soak the straw in water until it is bendable.
2. Spread the straw out on a covered work area.
3. Gather a little bundle of straw and trim it even at both ends. Bend it over so it makes a loop as shown in the illustration. Tie it to hold with red string. Do the same for a second little bundle of straw, tying it too. Make four bent bundles of straw.
4. Now arrange the bundles so the loops are all touching as shown.
5. Tie the four loops together with red string. Make a loop of red string and tie it to the straw decoration to hang the ornament from a window, wreath, doorway or Christmas tree.

Single Straw Ornaments

1. Explore designs and shapes made with single strands of straw. Weave, bend or fold the single strands of straw in any variety of ways, making different forms that might work for straw ornaments. See the illustrations for ideas or make up original designs. Spend as much time as needed exploring how the straw behaves when worked with.
2. When an ornament seems to be taking shape, tie red string around the straws to hold them in shapes or to join them to other straws.
3. When finished making the ornament, tie another red string around it to make a loop. Display the ornament by hanging it from a window, wreath, doorway or Christmas tree.

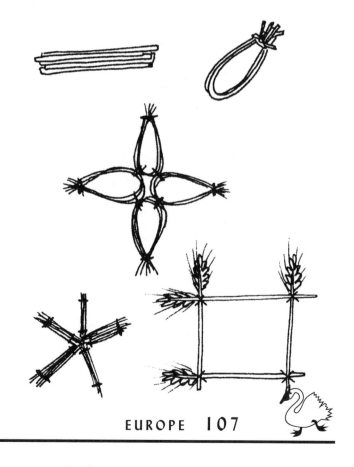

some experience   preparation   sculpture   caution

Sandbakelser (Sand Tarts)

SWEDEN

Did you know?

The people of Sweden are famous for their buttery bakery recipes. These rich Swedish tarts are shaped by hand into balls and then flattened and formed into any number of tart shapes. Sandbakelser are exceptional butter cookies—delicious to eat, fun to shape, easy to make.

Young artists bake Swedish Sand Tarts using molds or free-form hand shaping. This buttery recipe makes about two dozen tarts from 1" (3 cm) balls of dough. Double the recipe for double the delicious results.

Materials

½ cup (125 ml) butter or margarine
½ cup (100 g) sugar
1 egg yolk
mixing bowl, measuring cups and spoons
electric mixer, wooden spoon, spatula
sandbakelser molds, optional, from baking department of cooking stores
ungreased cookie sheet
oven preheated to 375°F (190°C)
toothpick, optional
drinking glass
spoon for making designs, optional

¼ teaspoon (1 ml) almond extract
1⅓ cups (200 g) flour
favorite jams or preserves, optional

Process

Purchase sandbakelser molds or hand-form the tarts. Both methods are fun and successful. First make the dough. In a mixing bowl, beat butter and sugar until soft and fluffy. Add the egg yolk and almond extract and beat well. Add the flour and beat well until mixed. Next, choose a molding method, either with a sandbakelser mold or by hand.

Strawberry Jam

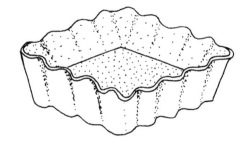

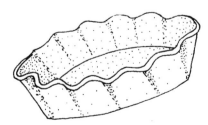

Sandbakelser Molds

1. Press the dough evenly over the bottom and up the sides of a mold. Place the mold on the cookie sheet. Repeat with all the remaining molds, placing them on the cookie sheet.
2. Bake for 8–10 minutes at 375°F (190°C) until edges are lightly browned.
3. Cool in the molds. Then, to remove, loosen the tart with a toothpick, if necessary. Lightly tap the molds to release the tart.
4. Eat as is, or fill with a little favorite jam or berry preserves.

Hand-Formed

1. Idea One—Form dough into 1" (3 cm) balls. Place on the cookie sheet and flatten with the bottom of a drinking glass dipped in sugar. Add additional designs with a spoon tip or toothpick. Bake and enjoy as in the above steps. (Let cool before removing from cookie sheet.)
2. Idea Two—Form dough into 1" (3 cm) balls. Press the dough into any shapes—flat or like little cups. The dough will change shape a little when baking because of the butter content. Bake and enjoy the delicious Swedish Sandbakelsers as above.

Spinach Egg Dye

SWITZERLAND

Did you know?

Every year as Easter approaches, Swiss children carry eggs to a town square in Zurich. There they compete to find the owner of the hardest, strongest egg—the one capable of denting all of the other eggs but remaining undamaged itself. Children often decorate these eggs with natural materials like small leaves and herbs, onion skins and other fresh plants.

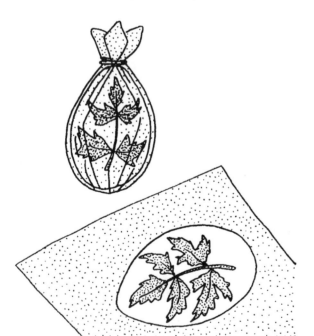

Young artists decorate eggs using fresh green spinach leaves to dye the egg shells and small leaves to form natural stencils. Finding the strongest egg may need to wait for another day and another egg.

Materials

scissors
old nylon stocking cut in 6 squares
6 uncooked white eggs
small leaves and herbs
6 rubber bands
1 pound (450 g) fresh spinach, or a box of frozen spinach, thawed
2 quart (2 L) saucepan with water and stove top or hot plate
slotted spoon and colander

Process

1. Cut the old nylon stocking into 6" (15 cm) squares, one for each of the six eggs.
2. Dampen some of the small leaves and herbs and stick them on an egg in a design. Do this for each of the six eggs.
3. After the eggs are decorated with leaves, place each one on a nylon square. Then pull the edges around the egg and tie the top with a rubber band to hold the leaves in place against the eggshell.
4. Put the spinach in a saucepan filled two-thirds full with water. With adult help turn on the heat and bring the water to a boil. Lower the heat to simmer.
5. Place the eggs in the saucepan of hot water, and simmer on low heat for 20 minutes.
6. Take the eggs out of the green spinach water with a large slotted spoon and place them in a colander. Run cold water over them until they are cool. Continue to run cold water over them while removing the mesh squares and peeling off the leaves. The eggs should be a pale green with the white shadowy stencils of leaves left on the shell.
▲ Note: To decorate more than 6 eggs, simply increase the size of the pot and the dyeing materials. Eggs can also be dyed in shifts, six at a time, using the same spinach water over and over.

North America

North America is a melting pot of rich and diverse cultures shown through the varieties of arts, crafts, inventions and celebrations across its continent. Each area of North America is filled with wonderful discoveries and surprises for children to experience through art. For example, young artists explore Canada Inuit Carvings, Caribbean Tin Lid Sculptures, Mexican Clay Sun Faces, Native American Coup Sticks and United States Canister Movies. Over 20 art activities are presented to help young artists explore the vast and diverse continent of North America's multicultural art.

Selected Bibliography

United States

Cowboys of the Wild West by Russell Freedman (Houghton Mifflin, 1985)

Dakota Dugout by Ann Turner (Simon & Schuster, 1985)

The Diane Goode Book of American Folk Tales and Songs by Ann Durrell (Dutton, 1989)

Hey, Al by Arthur Yorinks (Farrar, Straus, & Giroux, 1986)

I Go With My Family to Grandma's by Riki Levinson (Dutton, l986)

The Inside-Outside Book of New York City by Roxie Munro (Puffin, 1994)

Lewis and Papa by Barbara Joose (Chronicle Books, 1997)

The Rag Coat by Lauren Mills (Little, Brown, 1991)

Town and Country by Alice and Martin Provensen (Harcourt Brace, 1994)

When I Was Young in the Mountains by Cynthia Rylant (Penguin, 1982)

Who Belongs Here? An American Story by Margy Burns Knight (Tilbury House, 1993)

Mexico

Borreguita and the Coyote by Verna Aardema (Knopf, 1991)

Carlos, Light the Farolito by Jean Ciavonne (Clarion, 1995)

Going Home, Eve Bunting (HarperCollins, 1996)

Grandfather's Stories from Mexico by Donna Roland (Open My World, 1986)

Josefina by Jeanette Winter (Harcourt Brace, 1996)

The Little Painter of Sabana Grande by Patricia Markun (Simon & Schuster, 1993)

Music, Music for Everyone by Vera Williams (Greenwillow, 1984)

Pedro and the Padre: A Tale from Jalisco, Mexico by Verna Aardema (Dial, 1991)

Native American

Baby Rattlesnake by Te Ata (Children's Press, 1996)

Between Earth & Sky by Joseph Bruchac (Harcourt Brace, 1996)

Brave as a Mountain Lion by Ann Herbert Scott (Clarion, 1996)

The Buffalo Jump by Peter Roop (Northland, 1996)

Dancing with the Indians by Angela S. Medearis (Holiday House, 1993)

Dreamcatcher by Audrey Osofsky (Orchard Books, 1992)

The Girl Who Loved Wild Horses by Paul Goble (Simon & Schuster, 1982)

Giving Thanks: A Native American Good Morning Message by Chief Jake Swamp (Lee & Low, 1995)

In My Mother's House by Ann Nolan Clark (Viking, 1991)

The Legend of the Bluebonnet: An Old Tale of Texas by Tomie De Paola (Putnam,1983)

The Legend of the Indian Paintbrush by Tomie De Paola (Putnam, 1988)

Raven: A Trickster Tale from the Pacific Northwest by Gerald McDermott (Harcourt Brace, 1993)

Red Bird by Barbara Mitchell (Lothrop, 1996)

Inuit

Mama Do You Love Me? by Barbara M. Joosse (Chronicle, 1991)

Tikta'Liktak: An Eskimo Legend by James Houston (Harcourt Brace, 1990)

Very Last First Time by Jan Andrews (Simon & Schuster, 1986)

Caribbean

Baby-O by Nancy White Carlson (Little Brown,1994)

Caribbean Canvas by Fran Lessac (Lippincott, 1987)

Island Baby by Holly Keller (Greenwillow, 1992)

The Nutmeg Princess by Ricardo Keens-Douglas (Firefly,1992)

Hands Across America Paper Dolls

Young artists fold and cut paper into paper dolls that represent the peoples and cultures of North America.

Materials

thin paper (newspaper, newsprint or thin butcher paper work well)
pencils
scissors
colored markers
crayons (multicultural colors)
wall map of North America, optional

Process

1. Fold the paper into an accordion fold, starting with the short edge of the paper and folding it 2" (5 cm) over towards the center of the paper. Flip the paper over and fold this side again, always folding toward the center. Continue this procedure until all of the paper has been folded, back and forth, back and forth. If the end of the paper does not have enough space for a 2" (5 cm) fold, simply cut it off.
2. Hold all of the folds together and place on the work surface.
3. Draw half of a person on the paper area. Important: Draw the arms and legs so they touch the fold. If this is not done, the drawing will fall apart. Practicing first on some folded scrap paper or newspaper may help with the actual project.
4. Hold the folds together and cut through all sections of the paper, leaving drawn areas of the folds intact where the feet and hands touch.
5. Open the folds and see the outlines of people. (If they are not attached, study the area where a mistake was made and repeat the process.)
6. Color the features and clothing on the people, choosing to make each person different in clothing and skin color.
7. Make more paper dolls and attach the new set to the old set for a long chain of people. Add as many as desired. As an optional idea, display the dolls stretching across a wall map of North American, from one end to the other.

ALL COUNTRIES

Did you know?

North America represents the "melting pot of the world," a place where people from all over the world can live together, joining in work and play and sometimes building new families whose cultures come together as one.

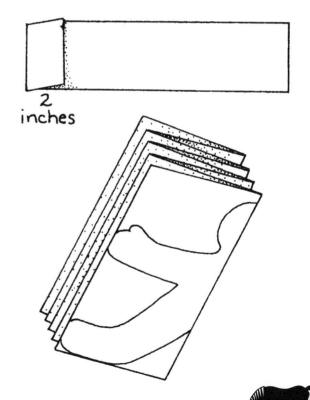

2 inches

Maple Leaf Print

CANADA

Did you know?

Canada's flag is white with a large red maple leaf in the center. The leaf design comes from the sugar maple, widely found in southeastern Canada. The sugar maple leaf is usually about 3–5" (8–13 cm) across and usually has five lobes that are separated by rounded, shallow indentations. Canada uses the red maple leaf design on their highway signs, on tourist attractions and everywhere they want to say, "This is Canada!"

Young artists explore the maple leaf design by making prints from a clay mold.

Materials

clay, or any play clay
fresh maple leaves with plenty of texture and veins (other leaves work well too)
pencil
tempera paint, Canadian red (other colors are fun too)
paper plate
paintbrush
paper

Process

1. Take a large clump of clay and work it until it is soft.
2. Roll the clay into a ball.
3. Flatten one side of the clay on the work surface.
4. Press a leaf into the flattened side of the clay. Press the veins and the outline into the clay until a deep impression of the leaf is made.
5. Peel away and remove the leaf from the clay. Look at the impression that is left. If desired, use the pencil to highlight or add more detail to the impression.
6. Pour the tempera paint on the paper plate.
7. Using a paintbrush, dab the clay leaf impression with paint, or press the clay gently into the paint puddle on the plate.
8. Then press the clay impression on the paper. Make several prints before more paint is added to the clay. Usually the second or third print is the best; the first is a good practice one.
9. Make as many leaf prints as desired. Change or add other paint colors to the plate.

Island Maracas

Young artists construct real, working maracas from burned out light bulbs and papier-mâché.

Materials:

light bulbs, burned out (2 for each child)
small stick or dowel about 4–6″ (10–15 cm) long
tape
wheat paste, water and bowl
newspaper
jars or cans, 2 for each child
acrylic paints, non-toxic
paintbrushes
Caribbean music on tape or CD, optional

Process

1. Tape the end of each light bulb to a stick, tight and secure.
2. Read the directions on the wheat paste. Mix the wheat paste and water in a bowl to make a thick, soupy consistency.
3. Tear small strips (1–2″ or 3–5 cm) of newspaper and dip them into the wheat paste mixture. Squeeze out the extra paste on the edge of the bowl. Then place each piece of paper with paste on it on a light bulb, overlapping edges, until the bulb is completely covered. Cover the area where the stick holds onto the bulb, too. Do the same for both light bulbs. At least two layers works nicely; three or four is great.
4. Let the covered light bulbs dry over night or longer, if necessary.
5. When dry, tap each papier-mâché light bulb against a wall or sidewalk to break the glass inside. Be gentle enough not to smash the papier-mâché shell. The broken glass will make the shaker sound.
6. Stick maracas in a jar or can to hold them up for the painting step. Paint the maracas with bright designs with the acrylic paint. Dry for several hours or overnight.
7. Shake the maracas back and forth to keep time and make a rhythmic percussion sound to music. If there is a recording of Caribbean music handy, play along!

CARIBBEAN

Did you know?

The Caribbean Islands are a rich mixture of cultures which include Indian, Spanish, American, French, British and African people. On the islands, music plays an important part of daily life, celebrations and religious ceremonies. The Indians from pre-Columbian times brought an instrument called the maraca to the islands. Maracas are still being used today.

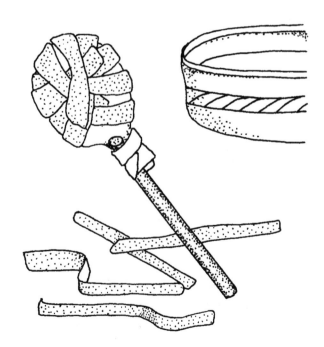

some experience   preparation   construction   caution

Bean and Seed Necklace

CAYUGA NATION, IROQUOIS CONFEDERACY, UNITED STATES & CANADA

Did you know?

The Cayuga Nation is a tribe in the Iroquois Confederacy. The Cayuga lived in the eastern part of the Iroquois territory in a section bounded by Canada in the north, Pennsylvania in the South, Ohio in the west and the Atlantic Ocean in the east. Today, none of the 450 tribal members live in this area, but rather are spread across the country. The Cayuga Iroquois are well known for their beautiful traditional beadwork, a highly respected art form.

Young artists create necklaces with simple beadwork patterns that might be similar to those made by the Cayuga Iroquois.

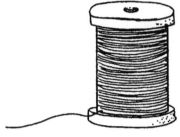

Materials

variety of seeds and beans, such as dried beans
vegetable or fruit seeds like corn or watermelon
bowl of water
large sewing needle and spool of strong thread

Process

1. Soak the seeds and beans in a bowl of water to soften. Some seeds will need to soak overnight. While the seeds and beans soak, think about the design of the necklace or bracelet and how long it should be.
2. When the seeds have softened, remove them from the water and poke a little hole in the middle of each one with the needle. A thimble can be very helpful for pushing the needle through the seeds.
3. Then dry the seeds overnight or until very dry.
4. Thread the needle with a piece of strong thread for a necklace or bracelet. Leave enough extra thread to tie the ends together after stringing the beads. (A stronger piece can be made by doubling the thread.)
5. String the dried seeds and beans on the thread in any design or pattern desired.
6. When the string is full, take the needle off the thread and tie the two ends of the string together. The necklace or bracelet is ready to wear or to give as a gift.

Scrimshaw

caution   drawing   preparation   some experience

Instead of using whale's teeth, young artists explore the technique of scrimshaw on a piece of a white plastic detergent bottle. Try scrimshaw on a clean, dry soup bone to explore bone scrimshaw, too!

Materials

white plastic dishwashing detergent bottle
scissors
sharp nail
charcoal or markers
hole punch
soft cloth
cord or string
dry soup bone, optional

Process

1. Wash out a dish washing detergent bottle until no suds remain. This can take longer than you think! Then dry.
2. With scissors, cut the top and bottom of the bottle away. More drying may be needed, especially inside. Adult help will be needed.
3. Next cut a piece of white plastic from the bottle to use for a piece of "whale's tooth" or "ivory."
4. Hold the plastic firmly on the work surface. Scratch a design into the white plastic with the nail.
5. Next, rub charcoal or markers over the lines to fill in the scratches. Then rub away the excess with a soft cloth or fingers. Go back and make more scratches and colors as desired.
6. Punch a hole at the top of the design with the hole punch. Insert a cord or string to make a pendant on a necklace or to make a loop for hanging.
7. Wear or display the scrimshaw. Make more from the rest of the bottle.
▲ Note: The next time there is a clean, dry soup bone around, try this same procedure on the bone.

GREENLAND

Did you know?
More than 85 percent of Greenland is covered in thick ice all year round. It is the largest island in the world and lies mostly north of the Arctic Circle. Fishing is a major industry, and in the past, whaling held great importance. Whalers developed scrimshaw, or scratching and engraving lines into ivory—whales teeth and bone. Ink was rubbed into the scratches, producing a picture. Through scrimshaw, whalers could record observations and stories they wanted to tell and remember.

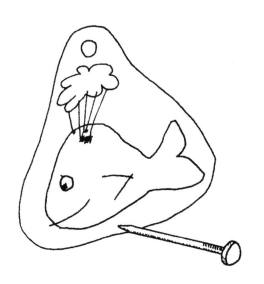

Inner Tube Stamps

HAITI, CARIBBEAN

Did you know?

Over 450 years ago on the sandy beaches of Haiti, Columbus found native children playing with odd-looking black balls made from the gooey, dripping gum of a native tree. Columbus took samples of the gum back to Europe. No commercial use was found for this gum until 1770 when Joseph Priestly discovered that it would rub out pencil markings. It was named "rubber" and became useful for many things, including inner tubes for tires.

Young artists recycle inner tube rubber into stamps, creating art prints.

Materials

old inner tube from a tire
wet rags for cleaning off rubber
markers or ball-point pen
scissors
white glue

small blocks of scrap wood for handles
tempera paints
grocery trays for paint
paper to print on

Process

1. Spread the old inner tube on the work surface. Wipe the rubber with the wet rag to clean. Clean hands, too, if necessary.
2. Draw a shape on the rubber with a marker or ball-point pen.
3. Cut the shape out with scissors. Draw and cut as many shapes as desired.
4. Glue each shape to a block of wood. (If letters or numbers were cut out, turn them over so they are backwards and then glue them on the block of wood. They will print correctly.)
5. Dry well so the rubber shapes will hold firmly.
6. Pour some tempera paints in the grocery trays. Use different colors in each tray.
7. Dip, dab or press the inner tube shape into the paint, holding onto the wood block, and then press onto paper to make prints. Several prints can be made from each dipping and dabbing of paint.
8. Change colors and make more prints. Dry.
▲ Note: Ideas for things to print are
   ✓ plain white tissue to make wrapping paper
   ✓ heavy note card to make stationery
   ✓ drawing board to make wall art
   ✓ paper plates, cardboard boxes or other surfaces for fun

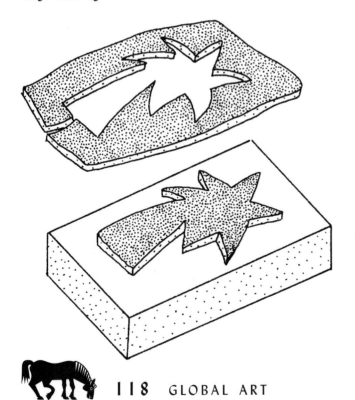

Tin Lid Sculptures

A common lid from a soup can or coffee can will function for recycling and creating metal ornaments for the young artist.

Materials

heavy work gloves
lid from a large can (coffee, soup or juice cans work well) or a canning jar lid
electrical tape or duct tape
woodworking table or other surface that can be pounded
hammer
items or tools to poke holes in lid, such as
   nails
   screwdriver
   chisel
   can opener
tin snips (scissors for cutting metal)
string or yarn
markers

Process

1. Put on gloves to protect hands while working with the can lid.
▲ Note: Extreme caution should be used when handling the tin lids.
2. With adult help, tape the edge of the lid with masking tape or duct tape to cover the sharp edge.
3. Place the lid on the work table surface. With the hammer and nail, pound holes into the lid to make designs. Pound or use other tools to make cuts and slits in the lid. (See illustrations for design ideas.)
4. Make one large hole in the lid for the loop of yarn or string.
5. Tie a loop through the hole, and hang the lid as an ornament.
▲ Note: The lid can be colored with markers, giving it a transparent color.

HAITI, CARIBBEAN

Did you know?

Haitians show their creativity by turning empty oil drums into musical drums, a popular form of music in Haiti. They also turn other metals into decorations and sculptures. Haitian sculptor George Liautaud is known for his metal sculptures of animals, mermaids, saints and other characters. He recycles metals into beautiful sculptured works of art.

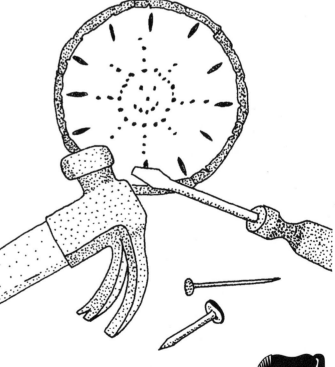

beginner

preparation
1

drawing

Yarn Art

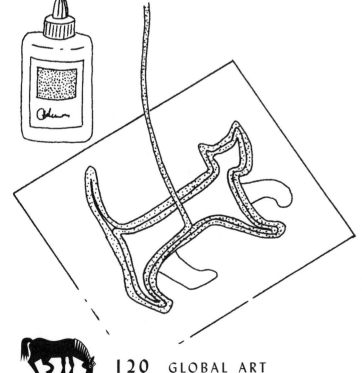

HUICHOL INDIANS, MEXICO

Did you know?

The Huichol Indians of the Pacific coast of Mexico create brilliantly colored drawings with yarn and wax which look like a painting when complete. Traditionally the art is used as a form of recording and telling stories and myths. The Huichol create their drawings by pressing yarn into wax on a board, then filling in the spaces with yarn so the design is bright and thick.

Young artists imitate the style of the Huichol by drawing with glue and then placing yarn strands in the glue lines.

Materials

cardboard square, any size—6″ x 6″ (15 cm x 15 cm) works well for beginners
pencil or colored marker
white glue in a squeeze bottle
yarn in bright colors
scissors

Process

1. Draw a simple picture of an object on the cardboard with a pencil or colored marker. The Huichol often use animals as central themes in their yarn art.
2. Squeeze glue from the bottle on the lines of the drawing.
3. Think of the strands of yarn as drawing with colored pencils or markers. Cut a strand of yarn and place it on a glue line. Cut more yarn strands or other colors and place them in the remaining glue lines. It's like coloring with yarn!
4. Fill in with more glue and strands of yarn, placing the strands as close together as possible with little cardboard showing through.
5. Continue gluing the yarn until the entire cardboard is covered.
6. Allow the yarn art to dry thoroughly, usually overnight.

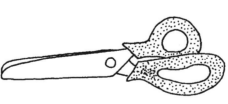

Inuit Carvings

The Inuits carve bone, animal tooth and ivory. Young artists explore carving a soft bar of soap into the shape of an animal.

Materials

large bar of bath soap, such as Ivory
pencil
carving tool, such as
     kitchen knife, nail
towel

Process

1. Use a pencil to draw the outline of an animal on the side of the bar of soap.
2. Use a carving tool to cut a little bit of the soap at a time, while shaping the animal form. Dampen fingers with water and smooth the soap as needed.
▲ Caution: Don't rub eyes with soapy fingers—it can sting! Soapy fingers in the mouth are an unpleasant experience, too. Also, wet soapy fingers are slippery, so dry hands often before resuming carving.
3. When the animal is completely carved out of the bar of soap, carve eyes and other detailed features to make the carving more realistic.
4. When complete, use the soap carving with water for washing or bathing. Or, save the carving as a work of art.

Variation

Soap Scrimshaw

✓ Scratch a design of an animal into the bar of soap. Fill the scratch with a bit of tempera paint or ink. Pat away excess color.

INUIT, UNITED STATES, GREENLAND & CANADA

Did you know?

The Inuit live in and near the Arctic, from the northeastern tip of Russia, across Alaska and northern Canada, to Greenland. The Inuit call themselves by words that mean "the people." In Canada they are Inuit, Yupik in Alaska and Yuit in Sibera. Because they must kill animals for food, the Inuit believe animal spirits may send them bad luck. To guard against this, they spend months carving the likenesses of the animals they kill as lucky charms and protection.

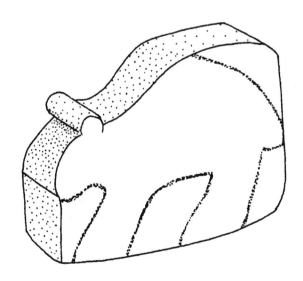

Clay Sun Faces

MEXICO

Did you know?

Mexico is known for its many clay pottery and art forms. Mexican artist Timoteo Gonzales is thought to be the first potter to make the unusual and delightful clay suns, so much a part of Mexico's tourist trade and folk art. These clay sculptures are called Metapec suns and are painted in bright, expressive designs featuring a variety of facial expressions.

Young artists sculpt Metapec clay suns, creating their own facial expressions and designs using any self-drying craft clay.

Materials

self-drying craft clay, such as Das, Pronto, Sculpey, Fimo or Crayola Modeling Magic
rolling pin
kitchen knife
bright tempera paints and paintbrushes
clear spray hobby coating, optional

Process

1. Work the clay by hand to soften it.
2. Place the clay on a work surface and roll it with a rolling pin to make a slab about the size of a cereal bowl.
3. Cut a circle in the slab the size of the desired sun sculpture. Keep the cut-away scraps of clay to add later for sun's rays and facial features.
4. Think of an expression to put on the sun's face. Sometimes it helps to make faces in a mirror noticing eyebrows, mouth shape and cheeks. Mold features into the sun's face. Holes can be cut for eyes, nose and mouth or added with more clay. Add designs and features to the face with the cut-away scraps. The rays of the sun can influence the expression of the face based on their design, such as straight, sharp, wiggly, thick or pointy.
5. Poke a small hole in the top of the sun for hanging it on a nail when dry.
6. When the sun's facial expression and rays are complete, allow the clay to dry until hard. Depending on the type of clay product selected, this is usually overnight.
7. When the clay is dry, paint the sun's features with bright tempera paints. Let the paint dry.
8. To make the sun sculpture shiny, an adult may spray with a clear hobby coating.
9. When dry, hang the sun face on the wall, on a fence or in a courtyard or patio area.

Easy Fiesta Piñata

sculpture · 2 preparation · experienced

Young children create papier-mâché piñatas and choose treasures with which to fill them.

Materials

old newspapers
container for newspaper squares
scissors
strong balloon
masking tape
liquid starch and aluminum pie plate

pin or needle to make holes
wrapped candy, small toys, treats,
paints and paintbrushes
art tissue paper
string
yardstick, dowel or stick from a tree

Process

1. Tear or cut the newspapers into about 1″ (3 cm) squares and place them in a container.
2. With adult help, blow up a balloon and tie the end. Tape the end of the balloon to the work surface with masking tape to keep it from rolling or blowing away.
3. Pour liquid starch in the pie plate. Dip a square of newspaper in the starch and stick it on the balloon. Dip and stick more squares of paper, covering the balloon. Try to cover the balloon completely with three or four layers, leaving the tied end exposed.
4. Then let the balloon dry well, sometimes for several days or overnight. When dry, pinch the balloon from the tied end and pop it with a pin. Pull the balloon carefully out of the news-paper form. Poke a hole in each of the two sides of the piñata to hang it.
5. Fill the piñata with candy, toys or other treats, or write up little coupons on strips of paper for gifts that can be claimed at a later time.
6. Cover the hole with masking tape or more newspaper squares dipped in starch (dry again). Be sure the punched holes for the string are left uncovered.
7. Paint the piñata with bright colors to decorate. Cut art tissue paper into shapes or designs. Press the art tissue paper into the wet paint on the piñata. Let dry for several hours.
8. Put the string through the holes and hang the piñata. Gather in a group. Blindfold one person at a time, and take turns trying to break the piñata open with a yardstick. When the treats fall to the ground, everyone scrambles to collect several for each person.

▲ Caution: Keep other children away from the blindfolded person trying to hit the piñata with the stick.

MEXICO

Did you know?

The piñata originated in Italy, but it is most commonly associated with Mexico. Piñatas were origi-nally made of pottery, but now they are usually made of papier-mâché. Everyone enjoys joining in the fun of taking turns trying to break open the piñata. When the piñata finally bursts open, the treasures inside fall to the ground, and everyone scrambles to pick up the toys and candy.

Framed Tin Plate

MEXICO

Did you know?

Tin plate art was developed in Mexico around 1650 when Spain restricted the availability of silver. Tin was an inexpensive substitute for silver and was used to create a craft unique to its soft structure that can be cut like paper. Today, Mexican artists often hand-color tin plate with bright dyes or inks.

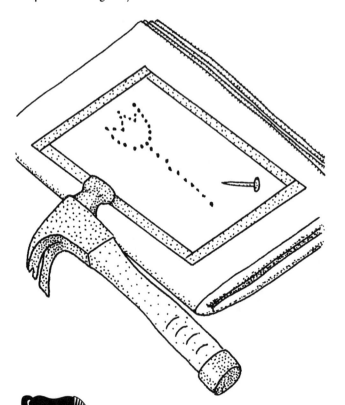

Young artists create a framed wall design using actual tin plate from a hardware or craft store. Aluminum pie pans or lids from large juice cans can be substituted when tin is not available.

Materials

work gloves to protect fingers, optional
tin plate, from hardware and craft stores
scissors
masking tape
newspapers
picture frame 5" x 7" (13 cm x 18 cm) with no glass

pencil
hammer and nails
window cleaner
paper towels
markers

Process

1. Put on gloves to protect fingers, if desired. If artists can work carefully, they may not need the gloves. Adults should supervise cutting steps.
2. Cut the tin to a size slightly smaller than 5" x 7" with scissors. Tin plate should cut easily, but the scissors may dull.
3. Put masking tape around the edges of the tin to cover the sharp edge.
4. Place the tin on several sheets of folded newspaper as a work surface.
5. Draw a simple design on the tin with a pencil.
6. Next, position the nail on the pencil outline and pound a hole in the design. Continue to pound evenly spaced holes on the pencil line until it is punched all the way around the entire design.
7. When the design is complete, spray window cleaner on the surface and wipe with a paper towel to clean the tin. Do not clean the back of the design because the edges of the nail holes are too sharp.
8. Color the tin design with markers.
9. Put the tin plate in the frame and display on a wall or shelf.

Sand Painting

Young artists create with bright colored sand and glue on heavy paper.

Materials

3 liquid fabric dyes, 1 tablespoon (15 ml) each, or powdered dye, 1 teaspoon (5 ml) each
hot tap water, bowls, spoons

measuring cup
fine sand
strainer
plastic tub containers
newspapers
wooden craft sticks

heavy paper, matte board or cardboard
marker
paper cups
slightly thinned white glue in a paper cup
paintbrush
white glue in squeeze bottle

▲ Note: The dyes are available in craft and hobby stores. Powdered tempera paint can be
  substituted for the dyes.

Process

1. For each of the different colors, mix the powdered or liquid color dyes with ¾ cup (175 ml)
   hot water in a separate bowl. (Using both dyes will produce brilliant colors.) More colors can
   be mixed according to colors of dye on hand.
2. Add the ½ cup (100 g) sand to the dye. Mix in. Let the mixture set for about 2 hours.
3. Place the strainer over one of the plastic tub containers. Pour the sand into the strainer very
   slowly and carefully to strain any water or particles. Do the same for each of the remaining
   colors.
4. Spread newspapers in three areas on a table, one for each color. Pour each color of sand
   out onto the separate newspapers to dry. Spread the sand out with craft sticks.
5. While the sand in drying, draw a design on the heavy paper with the marker.
6. When the sand is dry, pour each color into a separate paper cup.
7. Next, choose one color to begin. Paint thinned white glue into the area with that color in the
   drawing. Pinch the rim of the paper cup to make a pouring spout and carefully pour a small
   portion of sand on the wet glue. Let it dry for a few minutes.
8. Continue working with the glue and the colored sand until the picture is completely filled in.
9. To finish, squeeze a line of glue on the outlines of the drawing. Add a bit more colored sand
   on the lines only. Turn the paper sideways and tap away excess sand onto the newspaper.
   (Save the excess sand for more drawings.) Dry completely.

NAVAJO,
NATIVE AMERICAN,
UNITED STATES

Did you know?

Navajo medicine men of the southwest region of the United States
were taught to make pictures in sand
on a dirt floor. The pictures, they believed,
would cure illnesses and lift curses.

Paper Cuts

OTOMI INDIANS, SAN PABLITO, MEXICO

Did you know?

The Otomi Indians of San Pablito, Mexico make paper cuts from the bark of the amate tree. The Otomi believe their art will protect crops, keep away evil spirits, guard their homes and bring health to the members of the tribe. The cuts are symmetrical designs of people, animals, birds or other creatures they encounter in their daily lives.

Young artists use brown paper grocery bags to resemble amate bark and create symmetrical cutouts to hang in a window.

Materials

heavy brown grocery bag
scissors
chalk, pencil or crayon
newspapers
wax paper
iron
hole punch
yarn

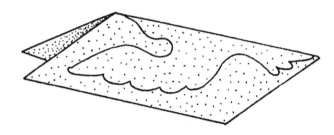

Process

1. Cut the bag open along the seam, then trim off the bottom of the paper bag. Cut a large square section out of the bag to use for the paper cut design. Save the rest of the bag to make more designs or for other projects.
2. Fold the paper square in half.
3. The next step will focus on symmetry, as shown in the illustrations. Draw half of the form of a bird, person, animal or other creature on half of the paper so it runs into the fold.
4. Cut the drawing out, leaving the fold in place. Do not cut the fold. Open the folded shape and see the symmetrical cutout.
5. Crumple the paper as if it were to be thrown in the trash. Then open the paper and smooth it. This gives the paper the look of bark.
6. Place a thick pad of newspaper on a table.
7. Place the cutout between two sheets of wax paper. Cover this with another sheet of newspaper to protect the iron. With the iron set on low and with adult help, iron the paper cutout until the wax paper adheres to the cutout and seals it inside.
8. Remove the newspapers. Trim around the cutout removing some of the extra wax paper, but leave at least a ½" (13 mm) or more around the paper design.
9. Cut a little hole at the top of the paper cutout and insert some yarn to make a loop for hanging. Display the paper cut in a window or hang from the ceiling.

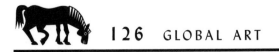

Salish Totem Poles

construction preparation beginner

Young children explore constructing a totem sculpture with cardboard boxes and paints.

Materials

cardboard boxes, from 3-10
tempera paints and paintbrushes
masking tape, duct tape
cool glue-gun, optional

Process

1. Paint the box with brown tempera paint. Dry completely.
2. While the boxes are drying, think of animals or characters to paint on the boxes that are going to be stacked to look like a totem pole. Ideas often used by the Salish are

| owl | crow | orca | clam |
| eagle | bear | cougar | salmon |

Other ideas from the artist's own environment might be

| dog | cat | fish | friend |
| relative | moon or sun | toy | car |

3. Begin stacking the boxes on top of one another to see how they will balance and how tall to go. For the purpose of stability, the lowest boxes will be larger and any smaller, lighter ones will be at the top.
4. When satisfied with the stacking design, take the boxes down.
5. Paint the boxes in the order of how they will be stacked, starting with the bottom box.
6. Let the boxes dry completely, usually overnight or for at least several hours.
7. When dry, start with the first box and stack the second one on top, using tape or glue to hold it. Adult help with the glue-gun is recommended. Add the next box, with more tape and glue. Continue stacking and securing boxes until the totem pole is complete.

SALISH, NATIVE AMERICAN, UNITED STATES

Did you know?

The Salish, a group of Pacific Northwest Native American tribes, created totem poles—poles with carvings of animal and human figures, each with a symbolic meaning. The totem poles told stories, gave information about the clan or family or told about the victories of wars or struggles with other tribes. Totem poles are only found in the pacific northwest of North America, dating about 300 years old in practice. Some coastal tribes, such as the natives in Port Chilkoot, Alaska, are re-learning the tradition and bringing back this lost art of their culture.

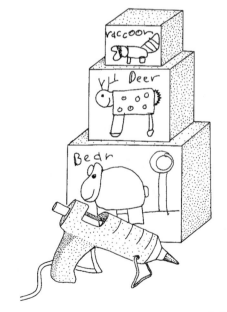

beginner   preparation   construction

Coup Stick

SIOUX, NATIVE AMERICAN, UNITED STATES

Did you know?

Over 100 years ago, the Sioux Indians did not write their stories down like we do today. Instead, they painted pictures on rawhide that would tell about important events in their lives and in the tribe. These rawhide drawings would then be tied to sticks called "coup sticks." The sticks were useful for retelling stories of the events gone by.

Young artists create a coup stick with cardboard, collage items and a branch from a tree.

Materials

large jar lid
markers, crayons, pencils
cardboard or heavy paper
scissors
paper punch
string or yarn
branch or stick from a tree (dowels work well too)
feathers, beads, buttons, ribbons

Process

1. Think of special accomplishments or events that have occurred throughout the year. Winning a soccer game, learning to ride a bike, a special holiday or celebrating a birthday are all good examples.
2. Trace a circle with the jar lid on the cardboard or heavy paper. Trace as many circles as there will be special events for the coup stick.
3. Draw a simple picture of this accomplishment on the circle. Draw one picture in each circle.
4. Cut out all the circles. Punch a hole in the top of each circle.
5. Now tie each circle to the stick with string or yarn.
6. When all of the special circles have been attached to the stick, further decorate the stick with the other collage materials such as feathers, buttons and beads.
7. Retell events of the year by "reading" the coup stick.

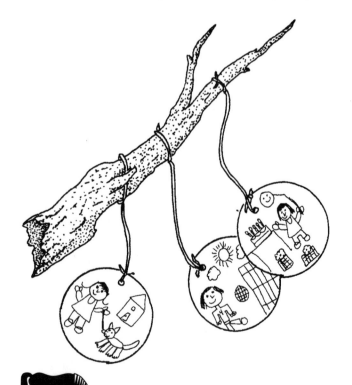

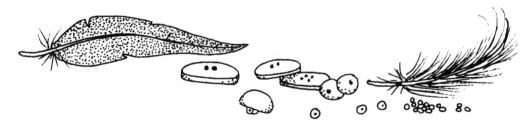

Calder Mobile

Young artists create mobiles with telephone wire, bits of paper and thread that stand and balance from a block of Styrofoam.

Materials

scrap telephone wire, about 2' (60 cm) long, or other pliable craft wire
scissors
block of Styrofoam from a packing box such as a computer would come in
scrap paper
glue and tape
thread, optional

Process

1. Ask a telephone installer to donate a length of telephone cable with colored wires inside. Open the gray coating and pull out the colored wires. Remove any threads that bundle the wires together. The wires can also be cut with scissors as needed.
2. Place a block of Styrofoam on the work surface. Press the point of a wire deeply into the Styrofoam. The rest of the wire can be curled or bent in any design to stand up from the Styrofoam.
3. Next cut bits of paper. Glue or tape them to the wire. (See the illustration.) As an optional idea, thread can be tied or glued to the wire and then a scrap of paper glued to the thread.
4. Insert another strand of wire into the Styrofoam. Repeat working with the wire and then attaching bits of paper to the wire. Insert as many wires into the Styrofoam as desired until satisfied with the sculpture.
5. Stand the mobile where moving air will cause the papers to blow. This mobile could also be displayed upside down from the ceiling.

UNITED STATES

Did you know?

American sculptor Alexander Calder is famous for inventing a style of sculpture called "mobile," meaning a sculpture that moves. Calder's mobiles either hang from the ceiling or balance on a stand. All mobiles require balancing and will move with air flow or wind.

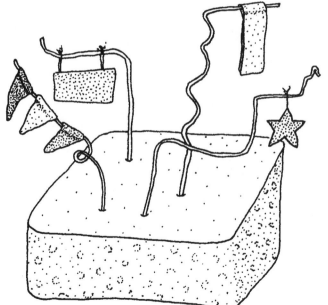

Apple Face Doll

UNITED STATES

Did you know?

The early settlers of North America made toys from natural materials and things they had on hand. People had no toy stores to go to and little money with which to buy things. The apple face dolls became a tradition that has remained part of the American culture, especially in the Appalachian mountains and New England.

Young artists carve a rough face shape into a peeled apple that, when dried, becomes the wrinkly face of a character doll dressed in scraps of cloth.

Materials

large apple
apple peeler and knife
baking sheet
oven preheated to 200°F (100°C)
oven mitts
fake fur, cloth and scissors
glue
pipe cleaners

Process

1. With adult help peel the apple, but leave some of the skin around both ends.
2. Carve out a rough idea of a face in one side of the apple with places for eyes, nose and mouth. Leave areas above and below the eyes and mouth for the forehead and chin.
3. Adult help and/or supervision may be needed for this step. Place the apple on a baking sheet and bake at 200°F (100°C) for most of one day.
4. With oven mitts, remove the apple head from the oven. It will be moist. Place it in the sun for several days to finish drying. The apple will shrink and a face will become recognizable.
5. Glue a piece of fake fur on the apple face's head to resemble hair.
6. Next braid three pipe cleaners together for a body. Then wind three pipe cleaners together and bend around the body for the arms. Do the same for the legs.
7. Cut a dress shape or other clothes for the apple doll and fit the clothes over the pipe cleaner body with glue to hold.
8. Stick the apple head on the pipe cleaner body and glue if necessary.
9. Although this doll cannot be played with like a toy, it can be displayed in many fun ways, such as sitting in a chair, standing beside a plant or as part of a crafted scene.

Early American Quilt Design

Young artists make a quilt design board as a wall hanging.

Materials

4″ x 4″ (10 cm x 10 cm) square of cardboard for the pattern
scraps of fabric
chalk
good scissors
large sheet of cardboard for the base, about 12″ x 12″ (30 cm x 30 cm)
white glue thinned with water in a cup
brush
wide ribbon, optional

Process

1. Cut a 4″ x 4″ cardboard square. This will be the pattern for building the quilt design. Other patterns could also be cut, such as triangles, diamonds or hexagons, but the square is the easiest one for beginners.
2. Trace the square pattern on fabric with chalk. Trace at least nine squares on fabrics of choice, watching for colors and patterns that go together or match.
3. Next, cut out the squares with good fabric scissors. Cut on the chalk lines.
4. Arrange the fabric squares on a 12″ x 12″ sheet of cardboard in a random or patterned design.
5. Lift a square of fabric. Paint glue on the cardboard. Press the square of fabric into the glued area. Then brush on and soak the top of the square with more glue.
6. Glue each square of fabric to the cardboard in this way.
7. To finish the edge of the quilt design board, glue a wide ribbon along each edge of the board. Ribbon could also be glued over the lines where squares meet. Dry the entire quilt design board overnight.
8. Display as a wall hanging.

UNITED STATES

Did you know?

Quilting bees, or quilting parties, were one of the favorite social times for women of the early American colonies. They would meet and work together, working on one quilt at a time until each person had a completed quilt. Quilting also made good use of fabric scraps; quilters developed simple and intricate unique American designs. Many quilt designs have been passed down for generations and are still being used today.

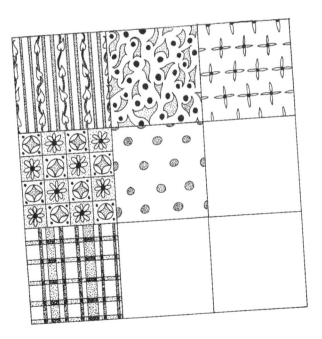

Photo Slide

UNITED STATES

Did you know?

Photography began with the discovery that exposure to sunlight turns things dark. Many experiments and discoveries with photography occurred in the mid-1800's, but it was not until 1889 that photography really arrived. It was then that George Eastman, an American inventor, invented the flexible roll film and camera.

Young artists design their own photographic slides and show them on a slide projector.

Materials

old 35-mm slides
bleach in a sturdy, shallow, non-tipping cup
box of cotton swabs
permanent markers, fine point
slide projector

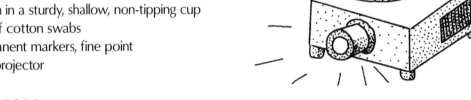

Process

▲ Note: Because using bleach requires caution, close adult supervision and help is needed for this step.

1. Clean the images off the old slides by dipping a cotton swab into the bleach. Slide the swab around on the transparency part of the slide, wiping away the picture that was there.
2. Clean the slide until it is perfectly clear. Then allow the slide to dry.
3. Repeat these steps for each slide. New swabs will be needed as they are used up.
4. Next, with the fine point permanent markers, draw designs or small pictures on the slides. Each slide can have its own unique art that stands alone, or the slides may progress in an order and tell a story.
5. When all the slides are complete, prepare the slide projector for a show. Music or narration is a nice addition to the slide show.
6. Show the slides on the projector.

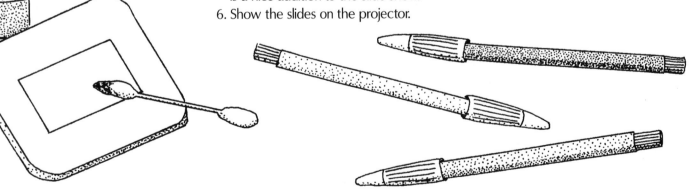

The Art of Hat Making

sculpture

preparation

experienced

The art of hat making has changed and evolved over centuries until the present day. Each young artist creates a hat from scraps and materials on hand—it may look more like a sculpture than a hat!

Materials

bowl for hat form
cardboard
ruler, pencil, scissors
aluminum foil, masking tape
collage and decorative items, such as

beads	buttons	confetti	ribbon
sewing trim	fabric scraps	paper flowers	cotton balls

liquid starch, small bowl, paintbrush
art tissue paper, in medium pieces
spray acrylic varnish

Process

1. Find a bowl about the size of the head of the person who will wear the hat.
2. Cut the cardboard into a 14″ (35 cm) square. Place the bowl in the center of the square and draw an outline of the bowl. Then cut the circle out of the cardboard square. Set the circle aside and save the square with the hole in it to use for the hat's brim.
3. Next, cover the rounded bottom of the bowl with foil.
4. Slip the cardboard square over the bowl within an inch or two (a centimeter or two) from the edge of the bowl. Tape the cardboard to the bowl. Use lots of tape to make it secure.
5. Pour the liquid starch in a small bowl. Dip a medium-size piece of tissue paper into the starch. Completely soak the tissue with starch so it will stick to the foil and the cardboard. Press the tissue paper to the cardboard rim or the foil mold on the bowl. Paint over the tissue with the paintbrush to smooth and flatten.
6. Completely cover the bowl and cardboard with tissue paper pieces. Paint any raw or ragged edges with more liquid starch. Let the hat dry completely.
7. When dry, carefully pull the hat away from the bowl form. Trim the edges of the hat brim.
8. An adult can spray the hat with clear acrylic varnish in a well-ventilated area or outdoors to make it shiny. Dry the hat completely, usually overnight. Wear as a work of art!
▲ Note: Other decorations like paper flowers, ribbons, sewing trims, glitter, confetti and beads can be glued to the hat to make it fancy and unique.

UNITED STATES

Did you know?

People all over the world wear hats. Some hats keep the wearer warm, some hats have a religious purpose, some hats indicate royalty or authority and still others are for pure decoration and fun. Hat making became a trade after a method of making felt was discovered in the 1400's. The first hat factory in the United States was established in Danbury, Connecticut in 1780 by an American businessman, Zadoc Benedict, and made beaver and rabbit skin hats.

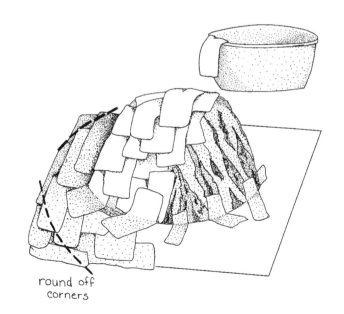

round off
corners

Canister Movie: Zoetrope

UNITED STATES

Did you know?

The United States is known for its film, cartoons and movies. But where did it all start? Optical toys such as the zoetrope contributed to the beginnings of the motion picture industry in the United States and throughout the world.

Young artists construct a zoetrope from a used, clean round ice cream canister. They watch a self-made movie of a dancing dot or other colorful design.

Materials

empty 5 gallon (20 L) cardboard ice cream canister, washed and dried
scissors or sharp knife
lazy susan (from thrift store or garage sale)—See the alternate idea for "spinning device"
heavy paper, 11″ x 17″ (28 cm x 43 cm), cut in strips about 5″ x 17″ (13 cm x 43 cm)
black marker (other colors are fine too)
desk lamp

Process

1. Wash and dry a five-gallon ice cream cardboard canister.
2. Mark the canister about 5″ (13 cm) up from the bottom all the way around. Then, with adult help, cut slots that are about 1″ (3 cm) wide, spacing them every ½″ (1.5 cm) or so, all the way around. The slots should be as regular as possible. Place the canister on the lazy susan.
3. Select a heavy strip of paper. Draw something in action for the entire length of the strip. An easy idea is to make a dot that goes up and down across the strip. Keep each dot fairly close to the next one. A slightly more advanced idea is to draw a little fish swimming along with bubbles and seaweed. Draw with heavy black lines.
4. Slip the strip into the canister with the pictures showing. Direct the desk lamp light into the canister. Spin the lazy susan and watch the movie!
5. Add color, work on the drawing a little and make any adjustments to make the movie work as well as it can. Once the idea is clear, draw more strips with more action and detail.

Alternate spinning device

Cut a piece of cardboard into a circle. Make a hole in the center of the circle, wider than the shaft of the nail. Put the nail through the circle and hammer the nail into a piece of plywood. The circle should spin. Center the canister on the cardboard circle. Then tape in place so the canister will spin smoothly.

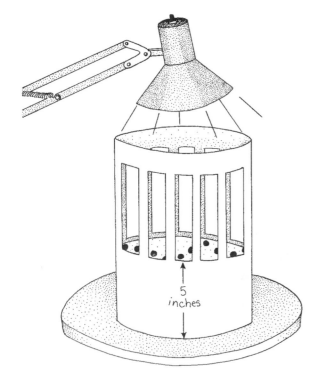

5 inches

Fraktur Certificate

painting

1
preparation

experienced

Young artists paint a Fraktur on newsprint to record an important event, such as a birthday.

Materials

tempera paints or watercolors
paintbrushes in various sizes (be sure to include some small, pointy ones)
large, plain newsprint

Process

1. Decide on a special event to record, such as a birthday.
2. On the newsprint, paint words that tell about the event, such as the name of the person, the date and any other information that might be of interest, such as the weather, who was present at the event, special gifts exchanged, special memories. This makes the certificate.
3. Further decorate the certificate with designs such as tulips, leaves and birds. Add any decorations desired. Vines, swirls of colors, geometric shapes as a border or dots and dashes are effective.
4. Allow the certificate to dry.
5. Display the certificate as a poster, use it to wrap a gift or make it into a book cover.

UNITED STATES

Did you know?

The name "fraktur" comes from the word fractura, meaning fractured lettering. As an art form, it is a hand-written document created by using flat, colorful, elaborate designs and disconnected letters. The early Pennsylvania Dutch people used Fraktur to record their passage through life with certificates decorated for birth, baptism, marriage and death. The certificate often doubled as a wrapper for a large coin that was a traditional gift given to a child. Fraktur designs use tulips, leaves, birds and other decorations.

Motion Picture Flip Book

UNITED STATES

Did you know?

The first motion picture was invented quite by accident. In 1872, at the suggestion of California Governor Leland Stanford, a photographer lined 20 cameras in a row at different intervals to photograph a running horse. Each was timed so it would go off when the horse's leg would hit the string. When the pictures were developed, the "motion" of the running horse could be seen in detail. This experiment led to "continuous action" photography and eventually to movie making.

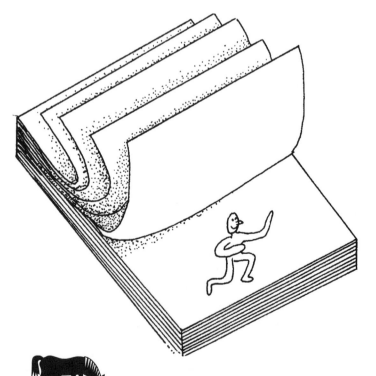

To see how this idea of pictures in motion works, young artists create a flip book with their own stick character.

Materials

small pad of unlined note paper or pieces of paper stapled together
markers or pencils

Process

1. Think of a simple stick character and something for it to do. For instance, a simple stick person running is a good beginning idea. A little dog or swimming fish would also be easy to do.
2. Start at the back of the pad of paper, because it will be flipped from back to front. On the last sheet in the pad of paper, draw a picture of the chosen character doing something, like a boy standing.
3. On the second sheet back, draw the same boy, but with a slight difference in movement, such as beginning to lift a foot to run. On the third sheet, increase the drawing to show just a little more movement.
4. Continue drawing the movement of the boy for at least eighteen pages.
5. Hold the corner of the pad of paper with the thumb, and flip the cards back to front to see the drawn character move in the "motion picture."

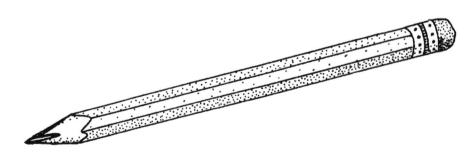

Oceania

Oceania consists of about 25,000 small islands scattered across the Pacific Ocean and one large body of land, Australia. Australia is the largest, along with the somewhat smaller lands of New Zealand and New Guinea. There are also thousands of tiny and medium-sized islands that may not even show up on a map! Some islands are crowded with people, some are empty, some are very large, others are just rocks. Since most of the islands are tropical, the artists of these countries use native materials such as grasses and shells to create their works of art. The art of these islands often combines music, dance and storytelling related to cultural or religious customs. Ancient Oceanic art traditionally used tools made of stone, bone, shell, sharks teeth and fish skin. Young artists explore the art of Oceania with projects such as: Aborigine Yabulul Story Design, Australia Koala Treats, Hawaii Paper Lei, Samoa Siapo Cloth, Tahiti Grass Skirts, Fiji Soft Coral Watercolor and Guam Chamorro Mat Weaving. The arts of Oceania are expressive in natural color and design unlike any other.

Selected Bibliography

Oceania

At Home in the Coral Reef by Katy Muzik (Charlesbridge, 1992)
Families of the Deep Blue Sea by Kenneth Mallory (Charlesbridge, 1995)
Life in the Oceans by Lucy Baker (Scholastic, 1993)
Magic School Bus on the Ocean Floor by Joanna Cole (Scholastic, 1993)
Night Reef: Dusk to Dawn on a Coral Reef by William Sargent (Franklin Watts, 1991)
The Ocean Alphabet Book by Jerry Pallotta (Charlesbridge, 1989)
Sea Shapes by Suse MacDonald (Harcourt Brace, 1994)

Australia

Dreamtime: Aboriginal Stories by Oodgeroo (Lothrop, 1994)
Singing Snake by Stefan Czernecki (Hyperion, 1993)

South Pacific

Call It Courage by Armstrong Sperry (Macmillan, 1939)

Yumbulul Story Design

Young artists can make up a story for a T-shirt design, just like Terry Dhurritjini Yumbulul, a great present-day Aborigine artist.

Materials

a story to draw	any white paper
fabric crayons	plain white T-shirt

▲ Note: Any plain white fabric can be used instead of a T-shirt, such as a

pillowcase	napkin	tablecloth	handkerchief

newspapers

iron set on medium (no steam), with adult assistance (follow directions on the fabric crayon box)

Process

1. Think of a story to draw for the T-shirt design. Tell the story to someone who can write. Listen to the story a few times. Picture the story deep in the imagination.
   Here are two examples of Terry's stories created for T-shirts he designs:
   ✓ The baby turtles hurry for cover in the protection of the coral reef. Here they can hide from predators. They share this home with small fish and stingrays that would have no chance of survival outside the protection of the reef.
   ✓ As baby turtles grow, they stay in the protection of the reef. Only when they get bigger and their shells become hard can they venture out into the open sea where they follow the currents and swim great distances before coming back to the reef to rest and feed.
2. Take fabric crayons and draw the story on white paper. Do not use letters and numbers.
3. When complete, spread the shirt out on a thick pad of newspaper.
4. Place the colored picture face down on the shirt. Cover the drawing with another sheet of paper or a piece of scrap fabric.
5. With adult help, press the warm (no steam), dry iron on the drawing. Follow the directions on the crayon box, pressing firmly and slowly.
6. Remove the drawing and see the art work transferred to the shirt.
7. Wear and enjoy the shirt. Wash and dry as any shirt. The designs will stay bright and colorful. However, do not use bleach.

ABORIGINE, AUSTRALIA

Did you know?

Full-blood Aborigine Terry Dhurritjini Yumbulul from the Warramiri tribe abides by the old tribal traditions and taboos, preserving his heritage in the form handed down to him. In his pictures and original designs on the T-shirts he creates the stories of his tribe, immortalizing animals, birds, reptiles and bush scenes. His art features the four shades important to the ancient aboriginal style of art: black, white, yellow ochre and red ochre, symbolic of the four major races of the world.

experienced   preparation   drawing

Mimi Rug

ABORIGINE, AUSTRALIA

Did you know?

Aborigines of Australia are known for the unique design work they painted on rock faces and eucalyptus bark in two styles. The X-ray style shows the internal organs as well as the outstanding external characteristics of animal or humans, usually done in more than one color. The Spiri style, or Mimi, shows human figures painted in one color. Many Aborigines claim that the Mimi or Spiri paintings are not painted at all but are shadows of passing spirits caught on the cliff walls. Both styles exist side by side on rock walls in Australia.

Young artists stitch a small rug on hardware cloth with yarn and a darning needle in the Mimi or X-ray style of the Aborigines of Australia.

Materials

masking tape
hardware cloth or soffit screen, with ¼″ (6 mm) squares, from hardware stores
yarn in many colors and large plastic darning needle
scissors
marker
toothpick

Process

1. Tape the edges of hardware cloth or soffit screen with masking tape to protect hands from sharp edges.
2. Cut yarn into comfortable lengths, about an arm's length for each strand.
3. Thread the large plastic darning needle with a strand of yarn. Or, if no needle is available, tape the end of the yarn to a toothpick.
4. Draw an Aborigine design on the screen with a marker, in either the Mimi style or the X-ray style. A kangaroo or koala are suggestions for X-ray designs, showing the bones and internal organs, using several colors. Any human form is a suggestion for the Mimi style, but only one color is used for the design.
5. Begin sewing through the holes in the screen with one color for the animal, design or figure. Add other colors as desired. When the animal is complete, begin sewing in and out for the background design.
6. When the entire piece of screen is covered with yarn, use it as a rug, a table runner or a wall hanging.

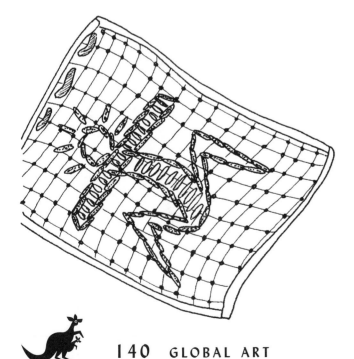

Dreamtime Painting

painting

preparation

experienced

Young artists paint their own landscape or animal design using dotted lines and many many dots of paint.

Materials

white paper
pencils
acrylic or tempera paints
paintbrushes

Process

1. With a pencil draw a landscape, animal or any imaginary scene on the white paper.
▲ Note: Aboriginal Dreamtime paintings often show animals from Australia such as turtles, birds, crabs and land features such as mountains, rocks and pools of water. The artist may wish to show animals or land features from his own environment.
2. Paint the design with lines, dotted lines, crisscrosses and many dots. This can take a long time. Fill the entire paper, but let the white paper show through the dots and lines.
3. Let the painting dry.

ABORIGINE, AUSTRALIA

Did you know?

Clifford Possum Tjapaltjarri is Australia's most prolific and world-renowned Aboriginal Dreamtime artist. Artists like Clifford paint stories from The Dreamtime, a time of creation and the underlying essence of all Aboriginal life and nature. Aborigines believe The Dreamtime is a track or path left by ancestral spirits. The Dreamtime is filled with stories now captured through art and usually composed of circles, ovals, straight lines, curved lines and many dots.

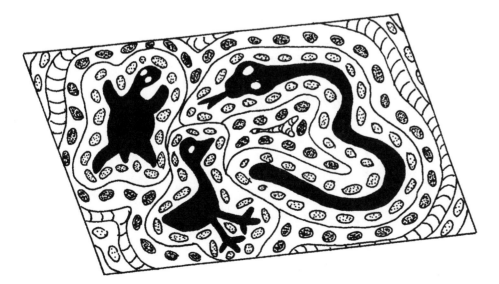

Koala Treats

AUSTRALIA

Did you know?

The koala is found only in the eucalyptus forests of eastern Australia. The koala are picky eaters, selecting only eucalyptus leaves and young eucalyptus bark. They look like teddy bears, but are more closely related to kangaroos, which are also marsupials. Marsupials carry their babies in a pouch on their abdomens where the babies nurse and grow until big enough to survive outside the pouch. Koalas are solitary, gentle and usually non-aggressive.

Young artists sculpt fuzzy koala sculptures from peanut butter and cocoa to eat as a sweet snack or party treat. Each recipe makes one koala, so double, triple or in any way enlarge the sculpting recipe for larger groups of children.

Materials

edible green leaves, such as lettuce or spinach
plate
1 tablespoon (15 ml) powdered sugar
1 tablespoon (15 ml) peanut butter
small mixing bowl
1 tablespoon (15 ml) powdered cocoa in a shallow dish
raisins or chocolate chips

Process

1. Place lettuce or spinach leaves, representing eucalyptus leaves, on the plate. Set aside.
2. Mix the powdered sugar and peanut butter in a small mixing bowl by hand. Knead and knead until completely mixed.
3. Make two balls from the dough, one for the koala's body and one for its head. Pinch off two more little balls for the ears (or use raisins).
4. Gently roll the peanut butter balls in the cocoa to make the koala's body and head look fuzzy.
5. Arrange the koala on the lettuce or spinach leaves like a koala climbing in a eucalyptus tree. Add raisins for ears, eyes and four feet.
6. Look over the sculpted snack, then eat and enjoy! Koalas are sweet!

Chamorro Mat Weaving

Young artists use crushed and softened strips of brown paper grocery sacks to weave a table mat with a basic over-under design.

Materials

brown paper grocery sacks, several per mat
scissors
masking tape

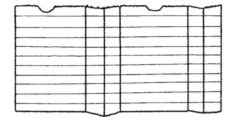

Process

1. Cut along the seam of a grocery sack. Cut away the base. Open the sack out flat.
2. Cut strips from the longest direction—about 2–3' (60–90 cm) long—from seam to seam (not top to bottom). Cut the strips about 1½–2" (4–5 cm) wide.
3. Crumple each strip, scrunching it and wrinkling it to soften so that it looks like a dried piece of palm frond or grass. Do this for all the strips, scrunching and unscrunching them to soften. Set them to the side of the work area.
4. Tape about eight strips of paper to the table. These will be the base of the mat.
5. Begin weaving a new strip through the strips taped to the table. Use the *over-under* method. Push this strip up against the top of the base against the taped edges. Leave the ends of the strip loose at each end for now.
6. Next, weave the second strip through the base, but this time use an *under-over* method.
7. Continue adding strips, weaving *over-under* and then *under-over* until the mat is filled, pushing the strips tight against each other. Use approximately six.
8. When the mat is filled, bend the ends of the loose strips around to the back and either tuck them into the weaving, or tape them down. Remove the taped edge from the table and tuck these ends in too or tape them down. Now the mat is complete.
9. Use the mat for a place mat or under a lamp, statue or other household decoration.

Variations

✓ Mats can be covered with clear contact paper to protect from spills and water, but they are prettier left natural.
✓ Mats can be painted sparsely with faint stripes or lines of darker brown paint to make the weaving look more like natural palm fronds.

CHAMORRO, GUAM

Did you know?

The native Chamorro people of Guam lost many of their native arts and crafts during the 454 years they were colonized by the Spaniards. One cultural craft that survived is pandanus weaving. The pandunus, or hala tree, native to the Pacific and Hawaiian islands, has such long aerial roots reaching to the ground that the tree appears to walk on straight, sturdy stilts. Pandunus leaves were used to make huts, canoe sails, wall thatch, window shutters, roof lining, garments and mats.

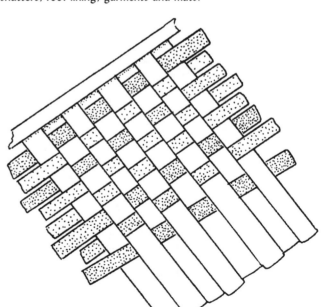

Stuffy Cod Hanging

FIJI

Did you know?

On Nananu-i-ra, an island of Fiji, Paul Miller, a resident of the island, keeps a school of tame sand cod, each weighing up to 45 pounds (20 kilos). Ben Cropp, one of Australia's best known underwater cameramen, has filmed amazing sequences with these large fish. These fish are friendly and come to be fed every day. They gently take food from people's fingers and allow themselves to be petted and stroked. Cropp wants to have the waters around the island declared a fish sanctuary.

Young artists construct a huge, colorful stuffed paper fish to resemble the 45-pound (20-kilo) cod that are hand-fed in Fiji.

Materials

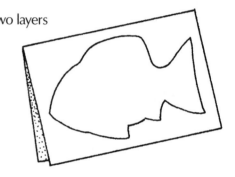

large sheet butcher paper, folded in half so there are two layers
pencil
tempera paints and brushes or markers
scrap newspaper or other papers
hole punch
stapler
yarn or string

Process

1. Draw a large, simple fish shape on the folded butcher paper. Make it large, round and full.
2. Cut out the fish shape through the two layers of paper. There will be two identical shapes.
3. Spread the first fish shape out on the table. Flip the second shape over so it is opposite the first (like butterfly wings). This way, both outside areas of the fish will be colored.
4. Paint or color bright designs on both fish shapes. They can be identical in design or styled completely differently. Dry if painted.
5. Place one fish shape on top of the other with the decorated sides facing out. The edges should match up. Staple them together around the entire outline. When nearing the first staple, stop and leave a large open space for stuffing the fish.
6. Wad up newspaper or other paper scraps and stuff the fish full of paper to make it puffy and full. Fill the fish as much as possible without tearing the staples out.
▲ Note: Shredded paper from a print shop's recycling bin is perfect for this job.
7. Complete the stapling and close the stuffing hole.
8. Punch a few holes in the top edge of the fish. Run some yarn through the holes to make a hanger and hang the big puffy, colorful fish from the ceiling to display and enjoy.

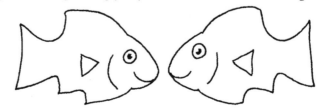

Soft Coral Watercolor

painting 1 preparation experienced

Young artists interpret the beauty and movement of the soft coral of Fiji through watercolor painting highlighted with outlines of permanent marker.

Materials

bare table or desk
heavy white paper or watercolor paper
masking tape
watercolor paints and paintbrush
jar of water
permanent fine-tip marker in black, purple or blue (fine-tip laundry pens work well)

Process

1. Tape the heavy white paper to the bare table, making a frame around the entire outside edge. (See illustration.) The paper should be flat and smooth.
2. Begin by painting very wet colors such as orange, pink and red to cover the entire paper. Use very wet paint so colors can blend and bleed together.
3. Fill the entire paper with blending colors.
4. Allow the paper to dry completely, usually for several hours.
5. With a permanent marker, draw outlines where the colors cross-over and blend, thinking of seaweed and coral shapes. Some areas can be left without outlines. The soft colors and the outlines will resemble the undulating, colorful underwater soft coral of Fiji.
6. Carefully peel and remove the masking tape and a natural frame will be left in white.

FIJI

Did you know?

Tavenui, known as Fiji's Garden Island, is the third largest island in the Fiji archipelago. Once known for its coconut plantations, Tavenui is now a famous landmark for scuba divers because of the coral reefs that fringe the island, and especially for its soft coral (*Dendronepthya klunzingeri*) which billows and undulates in the currents in dramatic, sometimes electric hues of orange, red, pink and white fringed with purple.

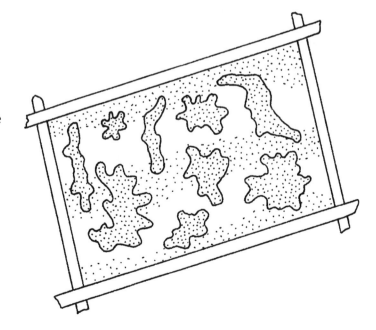

Aloha Paper Lei

HAWAII

Did you know?

In Hawaii, flower garlands or necklaces are called leis and were once made of feathers. Today most are made of flowers, but can also be made of berries, leaves, shells and seeds. Each island has its own style of lei that is given to people in the spirit of aloha, a sign of greeting, farewell, friendship or love.

Young artists construct a lei made from adding-machine tape that forms a pretty garland resembling a traditional white flower lei.

Materials

roll of adding-machine tape
scissors
tape

Process

1. Loosely roll a strip of the adding-machine paper so three or four fingers can fit into the hole in the center.
2. Hold the roll so the paper side, not the hole side, is facing upward.
3. Cut through the paper going slightly more than half way through all of the paper.
4. After the cut is made, bend the roll apart in opposite directions. This formation will resemble two eye sockets!
5. Hold the two eye sockets in one hand and find the ends hidden inside.
6. Start pulling the strips until there is a long garland or lei.
7. Tape the ends together and put it over a friend's head to drape over their shoulders as a sign of the spirit of aloha. Traditionally, a kiss on each cheek is given after the lei is placed around the neck of the special person.

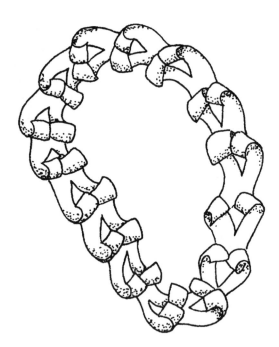

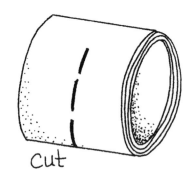
cut

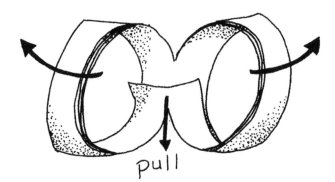
pull

Siapo Cloth

painting   preparation   experienced

Young artists create a siapo cloth from brown grocery sacks that have been softened by scrunching and unscrunching them. Designs are painted on the softened paper with black, white and brown paints.

Materials

brown grocery sack
scissors
tempera paints in black, brown, white
paintbrushes
▲ Note: Markers, crayons or colored chalk can be used instead of paint.

Process

1. Cut along the seam of a brown grocery sack. Cut away the bottom so it is one large sheet.
2. Wad up the brown sack into a ball. Squeeze it tight to make lots of wrinkles. Stand on the ball to press the wrinkles in deeply. Then unroll the wad.
3. Keep scrunching and unscrunching the paper to make it softer and more wrinkly like real siapo from uõa bark.
4. Spread the softened paper siapo on the work surface.
5. Paint designs similar to those from Samoa on the siapo. (See illustrations.) Samoan artists use geometric designs such as squares, triangles, diamonds and spinning wheel shapes, among many other designs.
6. When the paint is dry, display the siapo on a wall or tabletop.

SAMOA

Did you know?

Samoa is best known for its art called siapo, first created by Maria ★ Piritati. In Samoa, most art is done by women. The art of siapo is made from the bark of the uõa (mulberry tree) that is pounded into a large flat sheet. Then Samoan artists draw different designs on it and spread it in the sun to dry. The finished work is soft enough to be worn as a cloth and was used as clothing long ago. Now Samoans wear it on special occasions like weddings and community celebrations.

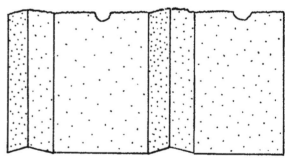

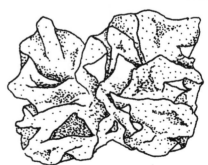

Grass Skirts

TAHITI

Did you know?

Tahiti is an island of French Polynesia. Tahiti was settled in 300 AD when Samoans established their first colonies there. Two centuries later, canoes from Tahiti set out for Hawaii and Easter Island, and in the year 1000, Tahitians colonized the Cook Islands and New Zealand. Thus, Tahitian culture is found in Hawaii and New Zealand and the other areas they colonized. Tahitian culture is well-known for the beautiful grass skirts, sometimes called hulas, worn by traditional dancers.

Young artists construct Tahitian grass skirts with raffia attached to belts worn about the waist. Dancing is a must, so dig up some Tahitian music tapes and enjoy the shaking grass skirts for boys and girls alike.

Materials

raffia

scissors

▲ Note: If raffia is not available, tear newspaper into long strips as a substitute.

old belt to fit around waist or hips

tape or CD of Tahitian dancing music

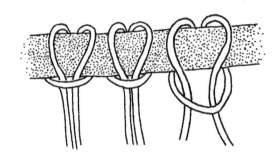

Process

1. Measure raffia from child's waist to the floor, and then double that amount. Cut at least 30 strands of raffia or more.
2. Pinch the center of the strand of raffia. Loop the center of the raffia strand over the belt and then pull the rest through, which makes a half hitch. See the illustration or simply tie on the belt.
3. Follow the same directions for all the strands of raffia, each one next to the last. This will fill the belt with long raffia grass.
4. When the belt is filled, buckle the belt at the hips or wear at the waist.
5. Shake the hips to move the grass.
6. Put on some Tahitian music and wiggle in rhythm. Add drumming sounds on the table or empty oatmeal boxes!

Variation

✓ Add some red pompoms to the belt area to look even more Tahitian. To complete the costume, wear shell necklaces or Hawaiian leis, a crown of flowers or leaves and carry raffia cheerleader style pompoms in each hand. A bathing suit or shorts make the skirt more fun to wear. Dance!

South & Central America

South and Central America are a blend of cultures, many that began thousands of years ago. Their arts reflect the old and the new, from the ancient Inca culture to the present day carnivals and celebrations enjoyed by all. For example, young artists explore Brazil Carnival Costumes, Ecuador Weaving Sculpture, Guatemala Sawdust Carpet, Quipu Knot Sculpture, Maya Ribboned Hats and Mixtec Codex. Over 25 art experiences are presented for young artists to explore the vast and diverse continent of South and Central America's multicultural creativity.

Selected Bibliography

Central and South America
Amelia's Road by Linda Jacobs Altman (Lee & Low, 1994)
Fiesta Fireworks by George Ancoma (Morrow, 1998)
Gathering the Sun: An Alphabet in Spanish and English by Alma Flor Ada (Morrow, 1997)
Grandmother's Nursery Rhymes: Lasnanas de Abuelita by Nelly Palacio Jaramillo (Holt, 1996)
New Shoes for Silvia by Johanna Hurwitz (Morrow, 1993)
Tortillitas Para Mama: and Other Nursery Rhymes by Margo Griego and others, (Holt, 1988)

Brazil
How Night Came to Be: A Story from Brazil retold by Janet Palazzo-Craig (Troll, 1996)

Columbia
The Monkey People: A Columbian Folktale by Eric Metaxas (Rabbit Ears Books, 1995)

Costa Rica
Fernando's Gift by Douglas Keister (Sierra Club, 1995)

Guatemala
Abuela's Weave by Omar S. Castaneda (Lee & Low, 1993)
Gracias, Rosa by Michelle Market (Whitman, 1996)
People of Corn: A Mayan Story retold by Mary-Joan Gerson (Little, Brown, 1995)
Sleeping Bread by Stefan Czernecki & Timothy Rhodes (Hyperion, 1992)

Panama
Grannie Jus' Come! by Ana Sisnett (Children's Book Press, 1997)

Peru
Tonight Is Carnaval by Arthur Dorros (Dutton, 1991)

Venezuela
Amazon Diary: The Jungle Adventures of Alex Winters by Hudson Talbott and Mark Greenberg (Putnam, 1996)

Fiesta Mask

Young artists create and design their own unique fiesta masks with a form made from clay and an impression taken with plaster of Paris.

Materials

newspapers or a tarp
modeling clay
petroleum jelly
large bowl and wooden spoon
wheat paste and water
tempera or non-toxic acrylic paints and paintbrushes
cord

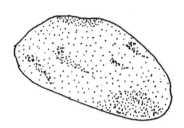

Process

1. Prepare the work surfaces with newspaper or a tarp to protect table tops.
2. Soften the clay and spread it out in a mound on a work surface. Model a human-sized face in the clay mound.
3. Prepare to papier-mâché over the clay face. Coat the clay face with petroleum jelly.
4. Mix the wheat paste with water according to directions on the box, until thick like oatmeal.
5. Tear pieces of newspaper into strips and dip each into the wheat paste. Lay the newspaper strips on the clay so they are about $1/8''$ (3 mm) thick, or several layers.
6. Let the newspaper dry thoroughly to set the mask. Then carefully lift the papier-mâché mask, separating it from the clay.
7. Paint the mask with bright tempera or acrylic paints. When dry, punch two holes, one on each side of the forehead of the mask, and insert a cord. Wear the mask or hang on the wall to display.

ALL COUNTRIES

Did you know?

For centuries, festivals—or fiestas—have been an exciting source of entertainment for the people of South America. Many villages hold fiestas in the name of their patron saint, and then spend many days honoring that saint with ceremonies, activities, music and food. A big part of celebrating during the fiestas is the wearing of masks.

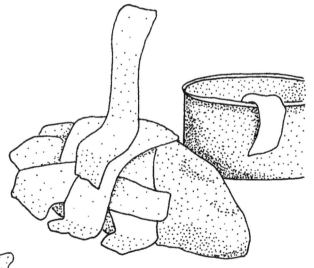

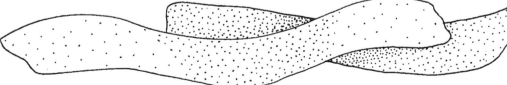

some experience | preparation | construction | caution

Three Kings' Cupcakes

ARGENTINA, COLOMBIA, VENEZUELA & OTHER COUNTRIES

Did you know?

On Three Kings' Day, families gather to eat Three Kings' Cake. This cake is shaped in a ring and looks like a king's crown. Its top is studded with jellied fruits like candied cherries and sparkling slivers of pineapple. Baked inside the cake are surprises like new shiny coins, tiny dolls or other small gifts. The first grownup to bite into a piece of cake with a gift inside hosts the party—and prepares the Three Kings' Cake—the following year.

Young artists bake Three King's Cupcakes from a yellow cake mix recipe. Each cupcake has a prize inside.

Materials

Ingredients

1 pkg. yellow cake mix to make about 12 cupcakes
1 cup (250 ml) water
3 eggs (save the 6 shell halves)
⅓ cup (75 ml) salad oil
powdered sugar in a small bowl
6 empty eggshell halves, saved from the 3 eggs
sugar cube for each cupcake
½ teaspoon (3 ml) lemon extract for each cupcake

Utensils

cupcake pan and paper muffin liners
small plastic toys, coins or party favors (If preferred, bake a big red cherry or a chocolate kiss into the cupcake for the surprise instead of plastic toys.)
mixing bowl
measuring cups and spoons
electric mixer or mixing spoon
rubber spatula for scraping bowl
oven preheated to 350°F (180°C)
matches
metal baking pan, for serving

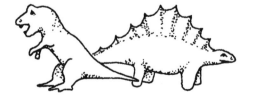

Process

1. Line the muffin cups with paper liners.
2. Follow the directions on the box of yellow cake mix to make the cake batter.
3. During the cooking process, save all the eggshell halves. Try to keep them in halves. Rinse them with water, and dry them upside down on a paper towel. Save for the "final touch" on the cupcakes.
4. Place a toy (or a piece of fruit or candy) in the cupcake cup. Slowly pour batter into each cupcake cup, covering the surprise. Bake at 350°F for 35 minutes or until a toothpick inserted in the center comes out clean.
5. Cool for a few minutes. Then, dip the top of the cupcake into the powdered sugar for a quick and easy frosting. Cool for another 10 minutes or so.
6. Arrange the cupcakes on a metal baking pan for serving. For the finishing touch, put a half eggshell, open side up, on each cupcake. Plunk a sugar cube into each eggshell. Pour ½ teaspoon lemon extract on each sugar cube. When everyone is ready, an adult lights the sugar cubes quickly and everyone can watch the flaming festive Three King's Cupcakes. The flames will burn themselves out. Then serve and eat.

7. Take small bites and chew carefully so toys are not swallowed! If children are young and toy represents choking hazard, cut cupcake in half so child can find and remove toy before eating. Happy Three King's Day!

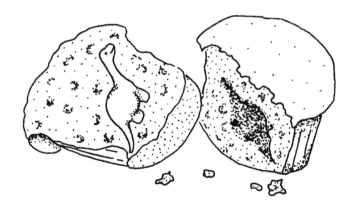

Aztec Sun Mask

AZTEC EMPIRE, CENTRAL AMERICA & MEXICO

Did you know?

Long ago, the Aztecs ruled a huge empire that flourished from Mexico through Central America. Everything about the Aztecs seemed to be centered in their beliefs and worship of the sun god, Huitzilopochtli. They believed their ancestors came from the sun, that the sun god would make the sun rise and set and that the sun was responsible for good harvest and general happiness in their world. They wore sun-god masks as part of their worship.

Young artists create a colorful paper mask that looks like the sun with a face to wear or display.

Materials

heavy paper or cardboard circle about 12" (30 cm) across, one for each mask
scissors
lots of scraps of paper from colorful sources, such as

construction paper	wrapping paper	magazine picture
Sunday funnies	paper punch holes	old colorful coloring book pages
junk mail	confetti	

newspaper-covered work surface
glue in squeeze bottle
glitter
string

Process

1. An adult can help measure where to make holes for the eyes (nose and mouth, too, if desired) of the artist, and cut out the holes. Poke two holes at either side of the circle for tying a string for the mask later.
2. Place the circle on a work surface. Spread out some of the scrap papers.
3. Cut scraps into squares about 1" (3 cm) big, but other sizes are fine too. Circles, triangles and odd-shaped scraps are effective. Confetti and paper punch holes will also work as part of the design.
4. Begin gluing scraps around the center of the mask first—around the eyes and nose and mouth—forming a circular pattern. Scraps can overlap, but spaces between them have a more authentic Aztec look.
5. Add more scraps around those, following the circular pattern. End with scraps forming a border at the edge of the circle.
6. Squeeze glue between the shapes forming a sunburst pattern or filling in all the open areas.
7. Sprinkle glitter over the glue lines. Gently shake excess glitter onto the newspaper to pour back into the glitter container. Allow the glitter and glue to dry, possibly overnight.
8. Tie string through the two holes and wear the mask. Is it a sunny day? Wonderful!

Edible Miniatures

Young artists work with a modeling mixture of mashed potatoes and powdered sugar to mold miniatures that are edible.

Materials

Ingredients

½ cup (125 ml) mashed potatoes
2 tablespoons (30 ml) melted margarine
1 teaspoon (5 ml) almond flavoring

½ cup (35 g) powdered milk
1¼ cup (150 g) powdered sugar, plus extra
food coloring

Utensils

2 mixing bowls and mixing spoons
sifter
refrigerator

small saucer
muffin tin and water
small paintbrush

Process

To make the dough

1. Put the mashed potatoes in a bowl. Add the margarine and mix well. Add the almond flavoring to the mashed potato mixture.
2. In a separate bowl, sift the powdered milk and the powdered sugar together. Mix the powdered sugar and powdered milk mixture into the mashed potato mixture.
3. Put the mixture in the refrigerator for about 3 hours.

To make the miniatures

1. Sprinkle some powdered sugar on a clean working surface.
2. Place the mashed potato mixture in the powdered sugar. Knead powdered sugar into the mixture until the potatoes feel like modeling clay.
3. Pinch off a piece of the mashed potato clay and mold a miniature piece of food, like an apple or a fried egg.
4. Now put several drops of food coloring in a small saucer. Try to keep them from running together. Have a muffin tin of water nearby to make the colors lighter and to clean the brushes. With the paintbrush, paint the food colorings on the miniature foods.
5. Put the molded foods in the refrigerator and chill. Use to decorate food dishes or as simple little snacks. Eat and enjoy.

BOLIVIA

Did you know?

A popular fair in Bolivia is the Alacitas Fair, held each January in honor of Aymara, god of abundance. During this time, Ekeko, who looks like Santa Claus without a beard, carries miniatures of things the people of Bolivia want or need. These tiny molded pieces might be sacks of rice and sugar, animals needed for farming, houses, automobiles or even clothing. The legend says that whatever Ekeko gives a person in miniature, the person will receive in real life.

Carnival Costumes

BRAZIL

Did you know?

The annual Carnival in Rio de Janeiro, Brazil was first held in 1840 and is now famous throughout the world for its elaborate, bright costumes. Prizes are awarded for costumes of all different kinds.

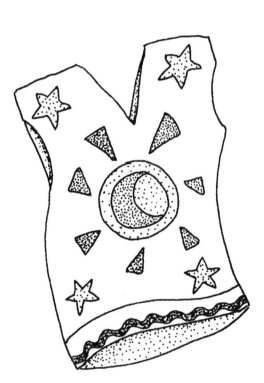

Young artists design their own costumes using a plain colored pillowcase as the base form and painting or sewing fancy details.

Materials

old plain colored pillowcase
scissors
newspapers
fabric paints and paintbrushes
miscellaneous trims, such as

beads	buttons	gems
sequins	sewing trims	ribbons

fabric glue
needle and thread, optional

Process

1. Cut a large "V" in the top (closed end) of the pillowcase, large enough so a person's head can go through.
2. Cut one semi-circle along each side of the pillowcase for arms to poke through.
3. Try the pillowcase on to be sure the holes work for the artist. Then take it off again to begin the decorating and designing.
4. Cover a work surface with newspaper to protect the table. Spread the pillowcase out on the table; put a sheet of newspaper inside the pillowcase. This prevents the paints from soaking through.
5. Now paint with fabric paints to decorate the pillowcase for a costume.
6. Dry overnight. When dry, add trims or decorations with fabric glue or by sewing. Dry again, if necessary.
7. Enjoy a festive parade and give prizes for costumes such as Silliest, Brightest, Scariest, Best Animal, etc.

Variation

✓ Add wigs, masks or face paint for additional costume fun.

Carnival Dancers

sculpture | preparation **2** | some experience ★★

Young artists sculpt a samba dancer from bendable wire and colorful carpet thread, a unique folk art technique from Brazil.

Materials

thick bendable wire, available at hardware stores
carpet thread, various colors
fabric glue
miscellaneous decorative materials, such as
    fabric
    felt
    tiny leaves
    beads
    sequins
    feathers
block of wood, hammer and small nails

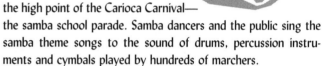

Process

1. Bend the wire into the shape of a human body. Be sure there is a head, torso, two legs and two arms. See the illustration.
2. Wrap the carpet thread around the figure starting at one end and winding around and around until the whole figure is covered with bright thread.
3. Give the figure more character by winding more but different colors around areas that can be highlighted on the figure. For example, wind red thread around ankles and arms.
4. Glue a variety of miscellaneous materials on the figure to give it more flamboyant costume detail. For Samba dancers, ruffled skirts, cuffs and collars are typical costume details. Add shiny beads and sequins with glue for added detail.
5. Nail the figure to the block of wood so it will stand.

BRAZIL

Did you know?

Carnival is Brazil's major holiday, and Rio de Janeiro has the best carnival in the country. In February, the city gets ready for the world famous event, featuring the high point of the Carioca Carnival— the samba school parade. Samba dancers and the public sing the samba theme songs to the sound of drums, percussion instruments and cymbals played by hundreds of marchers.

Drinking Straw Flute

BRAZIL

Did you know?

A Brazilian Indian plays an end-blown flute, an instrument that is found in every continent, but most particularly in South America and Asia. Known since pre-historic times, an end-blown flute is played by directing a concentrated stream of air against the sharp edge of the blow hole.

The young artist makes a flute from an everyday plastic drinking straw and then decorates it with feathers and colorful yarn.

Materials

plastic drinking straw
scissors
variety of decorative materials, such as
    feathers
    stickers
    colorful yarn
    plastic gems

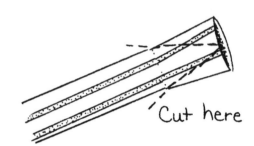

"Cut here"

Process

1. Flatten out about 1" (3 cm) of the end of the drinking straw. Crease the sides well so that it lays flat.
2. With scissors, trim the flattened end to a "V," as shown in the illustration, to make the flute reeds.
3. Glue a choice of decorative materials onto the straw to make it festive. Dry a little before trying out the flute.
4. Put the reed end of the straw in the mouth, just behind the lips.
5. Blow hard. Does the "horn" or flute work? Sometimes it is necessary to experiment with lengthening or shortening the reeds and with holding them in the mouth. But it's all very easy to do.
▲ Note: The shorter the straw is cut, the higher the sound will be, and the easier it will be to blow.

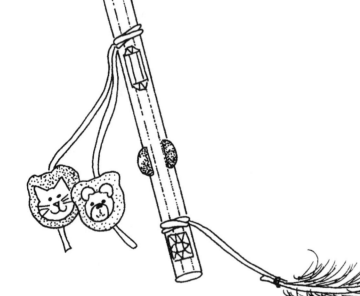

Hemp Rope Figure

caution   sculpture   preparation   some experience

Young artists work with hemp rope—a product of Brazil—to create a sculpture of the human figure.

Materials

hemp rope, about 2 yards (2 m) long
scissors
craft wire that will hold a shape (from a hobby or craft store)
wire cutters
block of wood, nails and hammer

Process

1. Cut the hemp rope into several 15" (38 cm) lengths.
2. Cut the wire into several 15" (38 cm) lengths also.
3. Stick the wire into and through one end of a piece of hemp, wind it around and around the rest of the entire length and then stick the end of the wire through the other end of the hemp. The wire makes the hemp bendable while still keeping its shape.
4. Wrap wire through the other pieces of hemp, repeating the above directions.
5. To make the human figure (or any other sculpture shape of choice), bend the hemp with the wire in it to form shapes like legs. Other pieces of hemp can be joined to the first by wrapping pieces of wire around them to join. Form arms, body, head and so on.
6. When the figure is complete, nail the feet to the block of wood so it can stand.
▲ Note: Some artists prefer to nail the first piece of hemp and wire to the block to give it a stand from the beginning.

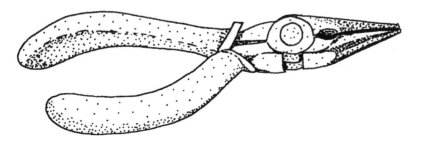

BRAZIL

Did you know?

In the 1700's and early 1800's, one of the best known Brazilian artists was sculptor Antonio Francisco Lisboa. He was also known as Aleijadinho, which means "little cripple," because he suffered from a disease that eventually prevented him from using his hands. He had to strap his tools to his wrists so he could continue making his sculptures. Today his works are famous and valuable. Since then, sculpture has reflected the region's Indian heritage, including monuments to heroes of wars.

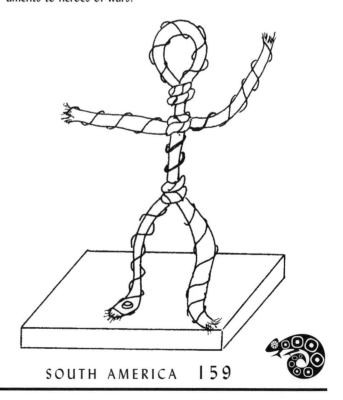

Fiesta Dancing Hat

ECUADOR

Did you know?

To celebrate the coming season of planting, natives in the mountains of Ecuador have an annual festival each winter with costumes and dancing in the streets. Part of the costume is a hat or headdress made of fabric and covered with decorations like buttons, ribbons and feathers. These hats usually have a tail made of streamers and ribbons that swings and sways and looks especially festive during the dancing.

Although the dancers in Ecuador are men only, young artists—boys and girls—can design and wear a dancing hat they make from collage items and sewing trims glued onto a paper bag-based form. Don't forget the streamers!

Materials

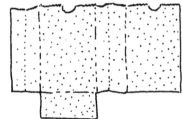

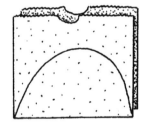

used brown paper grocery sack, one for each dancer
    and designer
scissors
crayons or markers
collage items and sewing trims, such as

feathers	buttons	sequins
sewing trims	confetti	ribbons
yarn	paper strips	

white glue
stapler

Process

1. Cut a brown paper grocery sack as shown in the illustration. Cut two hat shapes at the same time. Be sure the hat form is big enough to fit over a child's head.
2. Turn the sack hat patterns over to their plain sides. Decorate the hat shapes with all sorts of designs with crayons or markers. Lines that go across the design are effective. (Think about lines that are zigzags, fat dots or squiggly.) Any decorations are just fine.
3. Next glue on choices of collage items and sewing trims. Dry completely.
4. Staple the two hat shapes together around the curved edges, leaving the straight area open. Be sure to add some streamers.
5. Slip on the dancing hat and start dancing!

Weaving Sculpture

Materials

bowl
plastic wrap
white glue, water and any container, such as a cottage cheese cup
scissors
colorful wool or yarn
miscellaneous materials, such as

| string | yarn | feathers |
| ribbons | sewing trims | embroidery floss |

Process

1. Turn the bowl upside down. Lay plastic wrap on the upside-down bowl. This will be the form for colorful yarn strands and glue.
2. Mix equal parts of water and white glue in a container, like a cottage cheese cup.
3. Cut the wool or yarn into workable sections, about 12" (30 cm) long. Dip each length individually into the glue-water mixture and soak well. Remove any excess glue by holding the wet string above the container and pulling it through two fingers.
4. Now lay the wool or yarn soaked with glue on the plastic wrap.
5. Choose another yarn strand and repeat the steps above, soaking and then placing on the plastic wrap. Continue soaking yarn with glue and laying on the plastic wrap. Overlap the yarn strands but leave space between them for weaving between the strands.
6. When enough string has been used to cover the bowl shape nicely, set it aside and let dry for several days.
7. When the yarn is completely dry, remove the formed sculpture from the plastic wrap.
8. Study the openings where the string has not covered the sculpture. Weave the remaining materials—like feathers, ribbons and sewing trims—through the openings of the bowl-shaped sculpture.

ECUADOR

Did you know?

The people from Ecuador are famous for their weavings. Weekly market day is known as feria in the capital of Ecuador. During feria they sell their weavings, which are made of bold, geometric designs of brilliant colors of cloth. Weaving skills and abilities are passed down from generation to generation and are a source of great pride in Ecuador.

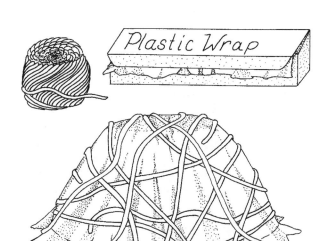

Plastic Wrap

some experience   preparation   drawing

Sawdust Carpet

GUATEMALA

Did you know?

In some cities in Guatemala, there is a beautiful custom during Holy Week. People spread carpets of sawdust along the route where there will be a procession the following day. These carpets are made of colorful sawdust sprinkled through stencil designs. They resemble richly woven woolen carpets and extend the length of a city street—quite a sight to see!

Young artists work with colored sawdust to create a sawdust design on heavy paper.

Materials

sawdust (free from lumber yards or wood shop classes), ½ cup (100 g) for each color
plastic bowls with lids, one for each color
powdered tempera paints, several bright colors, 4 teaspoons (20 ml) for each color
teaspoon and measuring cups
white glue in squeeze bottle
matte board or heavy paper

Process

1. Put ½ cup of sawdust in each plastic bowl.
2. Add 4 teaspoons of powdered tempera paint to the sawdust. Use a different color in each bowl.
3. Put the lid on the bowl and shake, mixing the paint into the sawdust.
4. Draw a design by squeezing glue from a glue bottle onto the heavy paper.
5. Sprinkle the different colors of sawdust on the wet glue, similar to using glitter.
6. Let the glue dry. Shake off excess.
▲ Note: To keep colors from overlapping, squeeze glue on a small part of the design, then sprinkle only one color with sawdust on that part. Repeat for each color.

Variations

✓ Cut a stencil from an old file folder. Hold the stencil over heavy paper. Paint some thin glue on the paper that shows. Without moving the stencil, sprinkle sawdust on the glue. Then remove the stencil. Shake excess sawdust away.
✓ Fill buckets with sawdust. Mix powdered tempera paint into the sawdust with a stir stick until the sawdust takes on the paint color. Cut stencils from cardboard. Choose a playground or large open area to create the sawdust carpets. Pour the sawdust over the stencil. Then remove the stencil with the extra sawdust. A design will be left.

construction   preparation   experienced

Young artists design a quipu with knots and strings to wear as a necklace, belt or to display, perhaps even coming up with a way to keep track of something that needs to be counted!

Materials

piece of heavy cord or twine, about 24″ (60 cm) long
chair
strings in varying lengths, from 6–24″ (15–60 cm)
scissors
masking tape

Process

1. Tie a heavy piece of cord, 24″ long or so, from one side of a chair to the other. Tie each loose end so that the middle of the cord stretches across in front of the artist. (See illustration.)
2. Take a piece of string and tie it to the main cord with a knot. Tie other knots in this string. There are many explorations of tying that might be fun to try, such as
   ✓ tie big knots and small knots
   ✓ tie knots up and down the string
   ✓ loop and double the strings over the main cord
   ✓ tie little pieces of string to the longer strings
3. Add more strings and more knots, eventually filling the main cord.
4. Wear or display the quipu.

Variation

✓ Select a string for each person in the family. Then tie one knot for each year that person has been alive—how many birthdays each person has had. For example, Mom's string might have 30 knots, Dad's 32 knots, Younger Sister's 3 knots and Older Brother's 10 knots. Have a string for pets, too! As the years go by, tie a new knot for each person as part of the birthday celebration.

INCA, PERU

Did you know?

The ancient Inca designed a system of counting and record keeping with brightly colored strings that had strategically placed knots called quipus attached to a base cord. The strings were different colors, lengths and thicknesses. No two quipus were alike. These highly complex counting systems were read by the quipu camayocs ("keepers of the quipus"). The ancient art of quipu is still practiced today in the Andean mountains of Peru, but most of the ability to read the strings has been lost.

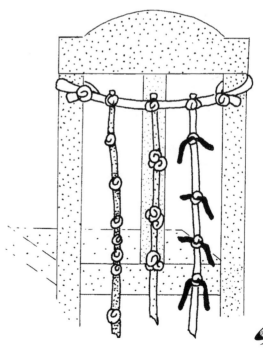

Ribboned Hats

MAYA INDIANS, CENTRAL AMERICA

Did you know?

The Maya nation is a native people that once inhabited the present-day countries of western Honduras, El Salvador, Guatemala, Belize, the Mexican states of Tabasco and Chiapas and the entire Yucatan Peninsula (Mexico). This civilization flourished for nearly 1000 years. Today there are 2 million Maya still speaking their language. At traditional carnival feasts, the men come attired in bright red coats and hats decorated with ribbons, in the style and magnificence of their ancestors.

Young artists capture the celebration of a Maya carnival by attaching bright ribbons to straw hats.

Materials

wide-brimmed straw hat (or any hat)
ribbons and other colorful streamer materials in bright colors (varying widths, lengths, patterns, textures), such as

| ribbons | yarns | strips of fabric |
| sewing trims | crepe paper | computer paper tear-offs |

ways to attach ribbon to hats, such as

| stapler | fabric glue | needle and thread |

scissors

Process

1. Select ribbons, yarn and trims to decorate a wide-brimmed straw hat. If a straw hat is not available, any old hat will do—baseball cap, wool watch cap, ski hat, etc. Or decorate a paper plate to wear as a hat!
2. Attach ribbons and other streamer-type materials to the hat with whatever method works best. Staplers work well around edges, glue and sewing work well on the more central area of the hat. Some design ideas are to leave ribbons hanging over the edge and to make loops and ruffles in any way desired. One suggestion: gather several ribbons together in one bunch; sew or staple them together, then attach the entire bunch to the hat all at once.
3. Let any glued areas dry.
4. Wear the hat in a parade, to a celebration or for fun!

Mixtec Codex

  2 preparation experienced
drawing

Young artists construct a folding codex with drawings and symbols that provide others with information about the artist's life.

Materials

white butcher paper, cut to 1' x 6' (30 cm x 2 m)
2 pieces of cardboard 1' x 1' (30 cm x 30 cm)
cup of strong tea or coffee, cooled and a small sponge
glue and tape
markers
ruler and pencil
watercolor paint and brushes

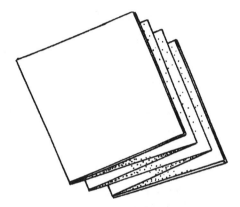

Process

To prepare "deerskin/bark" paper for the codex

1. Spread the butcher paper out on a table. Tape the corners down to prevent the paper from wiggling, if needed. Dip the sponge in the cooled coffee or tea, squeezing the liquid out on the paper in drops and pools. Spread the drops around on the paper, "painting" with the sponge to cover the paper. Leave some areas white too. Dry completely. Remove any tape. The brown stains will make the paper look more like ancient bark or deerskin.

2. The book will need to be folded back and forth accordion style. Measure every 12" (30 cm) on both sides of the paper, making little marks at each measurement. Fold the paper at each mark, first one way, then the other way like folded screens.

3. Glue the first folded square of the paper to a square of cardboard, to act as a cover to the codex. Glue the last page to the other square of cardboard to act as the end cover of the codex. Use additional tape to hold, if needed. Let dry.

To write the codex

1. Open the codex to the first page (the far right-hand page). Think of something to tell others through drawings instead of words. For example, tell the young artist's life history drawn from right to left with markers.

2. Add watercolor paints to enhance the artwork (and covers). Ancient Mixtec codices make use of rust-red, blue-green, golden-brown and soft-black, but any color is fine.

3. Display the codex opened and standing so everyone can read and enjoy it.

MIXTEC INDIANS, CENTRAL AMERICA

Did you know?

The art of a codex—a book of deerskin or bark paper that opens and closes like folding screens—is part of the amazing legacy left by the Mixtec Indians of Central America. Only 16 traditional codices have survived. These books display hieroglyphs and pictures that relate histories, the geography of the area, Mixtec myths or calendars. Each codex seems to be instructional, perhaps for the use of priests or rulers. The books flow from right to left with pictures in earthy colors of golden-brown, soft-black, green-blue and rust-red.

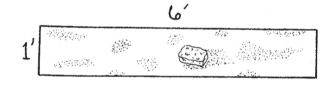

some experience | preparation | construction | caution

Fabric Cuts

PANAMA, SAN BLAS ISLANDS

Did you know?

The native peoples of the San Blas Islands of Panama are known for the appliqués with cut-out designs they create with colorful fabrics. The fabrics are layered and then cut away, layer by layer. Each raw edge is then sewn by hand, exposing each layer of color underneath the cut. These beautiful designs are considered an art but are also used in the home, as decor or for selling to the tourist trade in Panama.

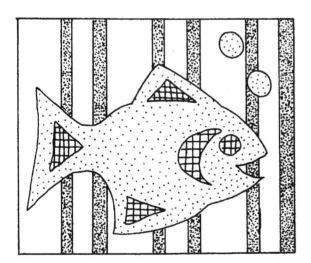

Young artists create a fabric cut design using any fabrics on hand with no sewing needed in this simplified version.

Materials

3 pieces of fabric, each with a different color or pattern, about 9″ x 12″ (23 cm x 30 cm)
matte board or cardboard about 8″ x 11″ (20 cm x 28 cm)
stapler or masking tape
chalk
sharp, pointed scissors
string, optional

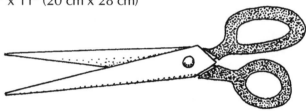

Process

1. Center the first piece of fabric over the piece of cardboard. Fold the edges of the fabric around to the back, and tape all the edges down. Stapling also works. Turn the fabric and board right side up again.
2. Center the second piece of fabric over the board and do the same, taping or stapling the edges down on the back. (For a simplified version, use only two layers of fabric and skip to step 4.) Now add the third piece of fabric, taping or stapling the edges down.
3. Turn the layered board fabric side up again. With the chalk, draw a large shape or design on the fabric. Draw several more shapes (at least three, but no more than ten). Shapes can be geometric, abstract or realistic, like flowers or hearts or animals.
4. With some adult assistance, poke the sharp point of the scissors into the top layer of fabric only (the third piece of fabric attached to the board) on the chalk line of a shape, lifting the fabric a little away from the layer beneath. Cut out that shape, being careful to cut only the top layer of fabric. This will reveal the middle layer. Then cut out all the other shapes in the same way.
5. Next, choose one of the shapes and draw a smaller shape in the middle of it. Cut out that shape, just as in step 5, revealing the third layer (the first piece of fabric attached to the board). Do the same for all the shapes, cutting a smaller shape from each one. The completed cut-out design will show the top layer with two other layers showing through beneath.
6. Tape a string on the back to use for a hanging loop, and display the art work on the wall, or place the work on a shelf and lean against the wall.

Anaconda Sculpture

construction   preparation   beginner

Young artists construct a huge anaconda snake from an old sheet and heavy wire.

Materials

old sheet
long piece of heavy bendable wire
heavy thread or yarn
fabric paints and paintbrushes

Process

1. Lay the sheet on the work surface.
2. Place a long piece of wire diagonally across the sheet from one corner to the opposite corner.
3. Gather the sheet around the wire to begin forming the snake's body.
4. Now wind the thread or yarn around the gathered-up sheet to make a long shape. Tie the heavy thread tightly.
5. Bend the long shape into a snakey creature, like an anaconda.
6. Paint the snake with yellowish blotches, or select colors and patterns of choice.
7. Let the snake dry overnight.
8. Enjoy moving the snake to different locations. For example, prop the snake up on a pillow, hang the snake from a doorway or arrange the snake on the banister or railing. Have fun owning a homemade anaconda!

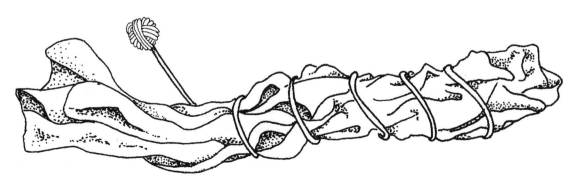

PARAGUAY & BRAZIL

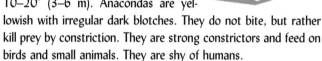

Did you know?

South America is home to the largest of all snakes, the anaconda. The anaconda lives in the water and can grow to about 50' (15 m), though more usually 10–20' (3–6 m). Anacondas are yellowish with irregular dark blotches. They do not bite, but rather kill prey by constriction. They are strong constrictors and feed on birds and small animals. They are shy of humans.

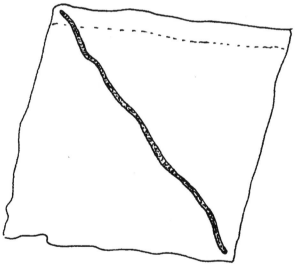

Etched Gourds

PERU

Did you know?

Beautiful, detailed works of art are made by decorating gourds, a squash-like plant with a hard outer shell. The people of the Peruvian Andes are well-known for making highly decorative scratched or etched designs on gourds. They are used as decorative containers and are also sold as sculptures.

Young artists etch designs into crayon colored on smooth gourds, similar to the carved gourds by the people of the Peruvian Andes.

Materials

soap, water, rag and towel
smooth, fresh gourds
for easy etching
  black crayon and cuticle stick
for true etching
  thick towel
  pencil or marker
  very sharp nail or other sharp tools, with adult assistance
  colored markers, watercolor paints or colored inks, optional

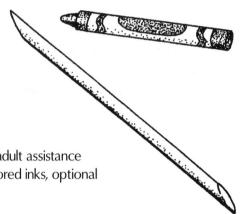

Process

Easy Etching

1. Use the rag, soap and water to wash the outside of the gourd. Then dry it well.
2. Study the shape of the gourd and decide what pictures to scratch into the gourd. Then color the black crayon very heavily all over the area on the gourd that will be "carved."
3. Use the cuticle stick to scratch away the color on the gourd, but not to cut into the skin of the gourd.

True Etching

1. Clean the gourd.
2. Study the shape of the gourd and decide what picture or design to carve into the shell of the gourd.
3. Cover the knees and lap with a thick, heavy towel, folded and doubled over. Place the gourd on the towel and secure.
4. Draw a picture with a pencil or marker on the gourd. Then, dig into the marks with the sharp nail (or try a chopstick sharpened in a pencil sharpener.) Experiment, supervised by an adult, with other sharp tools that will carve or etch the surface of the gourd. Work with the ones that work best for the artist.

▲ Note: Colored markers, watercolor paints or colored inks can be used to draw over the etched marks to color in the scratches.

Silver Wind Chimes

Young artists substitute aluminum foil pie plates for silver to make wind chimes that need just a little breeze to send musical sounds through the air.

Materials

1 large aluminum foil pie plate or jelly roll pan
different-sized foil pie plates or jelly roll pans
scissors
yarn

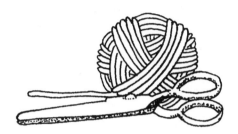

Process

1. Set the large aluminum foil pie plate aside.
2. Make a small hole near the edge of each of the other pie plates with the scissors.
▲ Note: Adult help and supervision may be needed to poke holes in the plates with the scissors.
3. Poke holes in the large plate, equal to the number of pie plates. Vary the positions of the holes.
4. Slip a piece of yarn through each hole in the large pie plate and tie a knot at the large plate end.
5. Attach the other end to a small pie plate and tie a knot. Do this until all the pie plates are attached and hanging from the larger one.
6. Make three holes evenly spaced around the large pie plate. Thread yarn pieces through each hole, then gather ends above the large plate and tie them in a knot together to make a hanging device.
7. Hang the wind chime from a tree or the eaves of the house. The pie plates hanging from the larger pie plate will blow in the wind, adding soft sounds carried by the wind.

Variations

✓ The pie plates can be cut with scissors into shapes and designs.
✓ The large pie plate can be cut with scissors to have an airy design with holes and shapes cut away.
✓ Hang foil plate shapes from a coat hanger or wooden stick as a mobile or wind chime.

PERU

Did you know?

Silver is a soft, white metal—one of the first metals used by human beings, as early as 4000 BC. Important silver mines were discovered by the Spaniards in Central and South America during the 16th century. Peru, in particular, is one of the leading producers of silver. Silver works of art and household items have become part of the culture and art of Peru, including jewelry, tableware, religious decoration, mirrors and coins. Wind chimes are one of the older silver works of art from Peru.

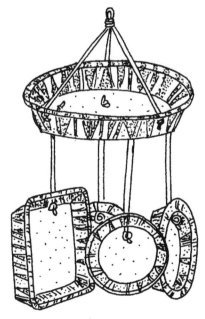

Indexes

Art Medium Index

Collage

Construction

Drawing

Experience level index

Beginner

Some experience

 ## Experienced

Preparation Index

1 Preparation 1— all materials are likely to be found in your home or school

2 Preparation 2—
all materials are familiar, but may need to be found or purchased before beginning the activity

3 **Preparation 3—** requires materials that may be unfamiliar but easily gotten, such as beeswax or window screen

Index of Terms and Materials

A

acetate 51
acrylic paints 75, 97, 141, 151
   See paint, tempera paint, watercolor paint.
acrylic varnish 133
activities for artists with some experience 13, 15, 17, 18, 19, 21, 22, 24, 26, 28, 44, 45, 49, 51, 52, 54, 60, 65, 66, 67, 72, 75, 77, 78, 79, 80, 84, 87, 92, 93, 97, 98, 101, 103, 105, 107, 108, 110, 116, 117, 118, 124, 125, 129, 130, 131, 138, 143, 144, 145, 150, 151, 153, 154, 155, 157, 158, 159, 161, 165
activities for beginner artists 16, 20, 23, 27, 29, 30, 31, 39, 40, 41, 42, 43, 50, 55, 56, 57, 58, 59, 62, 64, 69, 70, 71, 76, 81, 82, 83, 86, 89, 90, 91, 94, 95, 96, 102, 104, 106, 113, 114, 119,120, 121, 126, 127, 128, 141, 156, 166, 167, 168
activities for experienced artists 14, 25, 32, 33, 34, 46, 53, 61, 85, 88, 100, 115, 122, 123, 132, 133, 134, 135, 139, 140, 142, 146, 147, 160, 162, 163, 164

handkerchief   139
hardware cloth   140
hat   77, 164
   baseball   164
   straw, wide-brimmed   164
   watch cap   164
hemp rope   159
herbs   110
hobby coating   133
   clear   75
   clear, spray   122
hole punch   72, 80, 117, 126, 128, 144
   See paper punch.
hot plate   110
hula hoop   85

I

ice cream canister, 5-gallon   134
ink   168
   dropper top   78
   in a bottle   93
   oil based, non-toxic   78
   pad, red   49
inner tube   50, 118
insole, from shoe   50
iron   34, 53, 126, 139
   old   13, 92

J, K, L

jams   108

jars   115
jewels, hobby   25, 69, 91, 101
juice
   grape   93
   raspberry   93
junk mail   154
knife   121, 122, 134
lace   25
latex gloves   34, 78
   See gloves.
lazy susan   134
leaves   17, 25, 27, 31, 41, 53, 66, 71, 84, 110, 135, 142, 143, 146
   edible   142
   maple, large   114
lemon extract   152
lettuce   142
lid
   from any large can   119
   from canning jar   119
   from coffee can   119
   from jar   46, 128
   plastic or metal   71
light bulbs, burned out   115
linoleum floor scrap   50
liquid starch   123, 133

M

magazines   88, 154
margarine   108, 155
markers   16, 17, 22, 51, 59, 80, 85, 88, 100, 113, 117, 119, 120, 124, 134, 136, 140, 144, 160, 165, 168
   See crayons, paints, pencils, pens.
   colored   25, 65
   permanent   44
   permanent, fine point   65, 132, 145
mashed potatoes   155
masking tape   13, 88, 89, 90, 123, 124, 127, 133, 140, 143, 145, 163, 166
   See tape.
masks   156
matches   71, 152
matryoshka dolls   100
matte board   43, 78, 79, 84, 92, 97, 104, 125, 162, 166
   See cardboard and paper.
metal slab   19
metallic colored polymer clay   87
milk, powdered   155
milk cartons   88, 103
mirror   29, 102
   small   66
modeling beeswax   83
modeling clay   151
mud   26
muffin liners   152
muffin tin   155
muslin   67
   cotton   34
   unbleached   26

paste food colors 67

pastry bag 42

peanut butter 142

peat moss 103

pebbles 17, 57, 61, 64, 66, 103
  multicolored 57

pencil 17, 32, 34, 35, 46, 49, 50, 52, 54, 59, 69, 75, 79, 85, 87, 90, 94, 97, 98, 99, 113, 114, 118, 120, 121, 124, 126, 128, 133, 136, 141, 144, 165, 168
  See crayons, markers, pens.

penguin pictures 40

pens
  ballpoint 95
  laundry 145

petroleum jelly 151

picture frame
  with glass 84
  without glass 124

pie plate, aluminum 25, 58, 123, 169

pillowcase 51, 139, 156

pine cones 31, 70

pine needles 53

pins 123
  sewing or straight 41, 62, 94

pipe cleaners 42, 70, 130

plants 66, 103

plaster of Paris 14, 25, 33, 151

plastic wrap 15, 88, 161

play clay 114

playdough 59

pliers, needle nose 19

polymer clay, metallic 87

popcorn 43

poster borders 51

posterboard 102, 118

potatoes, mashed 155

potting soil 103

powdered milk 155

powdered sugar 45, 142, 152, 155
  See confectioner's sugar.

preserves 108

printing activities 49, 50, 62, 78, 104, 110, 114, 117, 156

R

raffia 34, 148

ribbons 69, 71, 91, 128, 133, 156, 160, 161, 164
  See sewing trims.
  wide 131

rice paper 62

rickrack 69, 94, 101
  See sewing trims.

rocks, small 64

rolling pin 17, 59, 89, 122

rope, hemp 159

rose petals 105

rubber bands 34, 35, 44, 71, 88, 110

ruler 25, 52, 61, 86, 94, 133, 165

S

sack, grocery, brown 143, 147, 160

salad bar container, clear plastic 71

salad oil 152

salt 39, 40, 62

sand 14, 55, 62, 64, 70
  colored 55, 101
  fine 125

sandpaper 13, 32

sand table 70

sandbakelser molds 108

sandbox 70

sawdust 162

scissors 13, 15, 16, 19, 22, 24, 28, 30, 34, 43, 44, 46, 50, 51, 52, 54, 55, 58, 59, 60, 64, 65, 69, 72, 80, 82, 90, 93, 94, 98, 99, 100, 101, 102, 107, 110, 113, 117, 118, 120, 123, 124, 126, 128, 129, 130, 131, 133, 134, 140, 143, 146, 147, 148, 154, 156, 158, 159, 160, 161,163, 164, 169
  sewing 77
  sharp 82
  pointed 166
  tin snip 119

screen, soffit 140

screens, for painting 53

sculpture activities 14, 15, 18, 19, 23, 24, 25, 33, 40, 42, 43, 45, 57, 59, 61, 70, 81, 83, 86, 87, 104, 105, 108, 118, 120, 121, 122, 126, 128, 129, 132, 141, 150, 154, 155, 158, 160

telephone wire   129

tempera paints   20, 29, 33, 40, 50, 51, 62, 88,
    89, 92, 95, 104, 114, 118, 122, 127, 135,
    141, 144, 147, 162
    See paints, watercolor paints, acrylic paints.
    liquid only   56
    powdered only   55

thread   34, 54, 129, 156, 164.
    See cord, string, rope, yarn
    carpet   157
    heavy   167
    metallic   101
    strong   116

tiles, bisque   106

tin plate   124

tin snips   119

leaves   157

tissue paper   118

tissues   29, 56

tools   108
    carving   121
    etching   49, 95, 168
    kitchen   59
    poking   119
    sculpting   14

toothbrush   41

toothpick   84, 140
    round   18

toys   70
    figurine   66
    pieces   59

plastic, small   152
    small   123

tray   55, 61

treats   123

T-shirt, plain white   139

tubs, plastic   125

twigs   25, 31

twine   163

V, W, Y

varnish
    acrylic   133
    plastic   75

vest   77

vinegar   76

wading pool   71

wallpaper   51

water bottle, spray or misting   64

water table   71

wax paper   21, 92, 126

weeds   17, 31, 70, 84

wheat paste   115, 151

white bread   86

wigs   156

window cleaner   124

wire
    bendable   157, 167
    brass or copper, heavy   19
    craft   129, 159
    telephone cable, colored   19, 24, 129

wire cutter   19, 159

wood
    block   157, 159
    scraps   50, 71, 118

wooden board   97

woodworking table   119

wool   161

wrapping paper   51, 118
    See paper.

yardstick   123

yarn   28, 69, 119, 120, 126, 128, 140, 158,
    160, 161, 164, 167, 169
    See string, cord, thread, twine.

Index of Activities by Country or Continent

(When activities reflect multiple countries, they are listed under each country.)

Alphabetical Activity List

Cooking Art
Easy Edible Art for Young Children

MaryAnn Kohl and Jean Potter

Transform the kitchen into an artist's studio with these easy edible art experiences. Organized by theme, such as Shapes & Forms and Color & Design, Cooking Art combines the familiar area of art exploration with the fascinating world of cooking including all of its wondrous tools, tastes and outcomes. Includes recipes for snacks, sandwiches, drinks, desserts, breads, fruit as well as pet treats. Each recipe allows ample room for cooking artists to explore and create in their own special, unique ways. 192 pages. 1997.

ISBN 0-87659-184-5 / Gryphon House
18237 / Paperback

Math Arts
Exploring Math through Art for 3 to 6 Year Olds

MaryAnn Kohl and Cindy Gainer

Get ready to create and count in this exciting introduction to math! This innovative approach uses creative art projects to introduce early math concepts. Each of the 200 hands-on projects is designed to help children discover essential math skills through a creative process unique to every individual. This well organized book provides both teachers and parents with a diverse range of activities for making math both fun and fascinating. The possibilities are endless! 256 pages. 1996.

ISBN 0-87659-177-2 / Gryphon House
16987 / Paperback

Preschool Art

It's the Process, Not the Product

MaryAnn Kohl

Anyone working with preschoolers and early primary age children will want this book. Over 200 activities teach children to explore and understand their world through open-ended art experiences that emphasize the process of art, not the product. The first chapter introduces basic art activities appropriate for all children, while subsequent chapters, which build on the activities in the first chapter, are divided by seasons. With activities that include painting, drawing, collage, sculpture and construction, this is the only art book you will need. 260 pages.

ISBN 0-87659-168-3 / Gryphon House
16985 / Paperback